T0304335

THE
REACTIONARY
SPIRIT

THE

REACTIONARY
SPIRIT

HOW AMERICA'S MOST INSIDIOUS
POLITICAL TRADITION SWEPT THE WORLD

ZACK BEAUCHAMP

PUBLICAFFAIRS
New York

PublicAffairs
Hachette Book Group
1290 Avenue of the Americas, New York, NY 10104
www.publicaffairsbooks.com
@Public_Affairs

Printed in the United States of America

First Edition: July 2024

Published by PublicAffairs, an imprint of Hachette Book Group, Inc. The PublicAffairs name and logo is a registered trademark of the Hachette Book Group.

The Hachette Speakers Bureau provides a wide range of authors for speaking events. To find out more, go to hachettespeakersbureau.com or email HachetteSpeakers@hbgusa.com.

PublicAffairs books may be purchased in bulk for business, educational, or promotional use. For more information, please contact your local bookseller or the Hachette Book Group Special Markets Department at special.markets@hbgusa.com.

The publisher is not responsible for websites (or their content) that are not owned by the publisher.

Print book interior design by Bart Dawson.

Library of Congress Cataloging-in-Publication Data

Names: Beauchamp, Zack, author.
Title: The reactionary spirit : how America's most insidious political tradition swept the world / Zack Beauchamp.
Description: First edition. | New York, N.Y. : PublicAffairs, 2024. | Includes bibliographical references and index. |
Identifiers: LCCN 2023056316 | ISBN 9781541704411 (hardcover) | ISBN 9781541704435 (ebook)
Subjects: LCSH: Political culture—United States. | Authoritarianism. | Democratization. | United States—Politics and government—21st century. | Hungary—Politics and government—21st century. | Israel—Politics and government—21st century. | India—Politics and government—21st century. | China—Politics and government—21st century. | World politics—21st century.
Classification: LCC JK1726 .B435 2024 | DDC 306.20973—dc23/eng/20240222
LC record available at https://lccn.loc.gov/2023056316

ISBNs: 9781541704411 (hardcover); 9781541704435 (ebook)

LSC-C

Printing 1, 2024

To my father, for showing me the way

As I would not be a slave, so I would not be a master. This expresses my idea of democracy.

—Abraham Lincoln, *Definition of Democracy*

The doctrine of equality! . . . But there is no more poisonous poison.

—Friedrich Nietzsche, *Twilight of the Idols*

CONTENTS

INTRODUCTION

In March 2013, I went to the Gaylord National Resort and Convention Center, a hulking indoor facility located just south of Washington, DC, and saw the stirrings of a democratic crisis. The Gaylord was playing host to the Conservative Political Action Conference (CPAC), the flagship gathering of the American political right. At the time, the GOP was still shaped by a Tea Party aesthetic: CPAC attendees donned tricorn hats and waved Gadsden flags in the manner of the anti-Obama protesters who had risen up four years prior.

My primary job at the conference was to document, as best I could, the extremism that was taking root in the GOP. I was a cub reporter at a liberal blog, so Republican politicians weren't exactly lining up to talk to me. I would chase them down the hallways, shouting questions, usually getting only deflections or stony silence. Another tack proved more fruitful: attending the conference's smaller breakout sessions to see what the speakers and attendees said when they were in a safe space.

A colleague and I settled in at a session titled "Trump the Race Card." While any presentation with that title today would be about Donald, this one wasn't (though Trump did speak at the conference). The session was headlined by a man named K. Carl Smith, founder of the Frederick Douglass Republicans, an outfit that purported to sell conservative ideas to Black audiences. After Smith worked his way through his presentation, a man with a buzz cut and thin beard stood up to ask a question. He identified himself as Scott Terry, from North Carolina.

"It seems to me that you're reaching out to voters—the method, the program you're offering us—at the expense of young, white Southern males like myself," Terry said. Hearing this, I immediately started filming the panel on my phone.

"I feel like my people, my demographic, are being systematically disenfranchised," Terry continued. "Why can't we be more like Booker T. Washington Republicans, and his famous statement: 'Let's be unified like the hand, but separate like the fingers.'"

The line comes from Washington's address at an agricultural and cultural fair in Atlanta in 1895, where the leading Black intellectual offered whites a compromise: help improve the economic status of the Black population, and they would tolerate segregation and political disenfranchisement. Washington was trying to do what he could for a profoundly vulnerable community. Reconstruction had recently ended, and ascendant Southern whites were busy constructing the Jim Crow political order. Scott Terry did not see segregation as a terrible short-term inevitability that must ultimately end, as Washington did, but as an affirmative ideal—a policy the country should return to today.

It wasn't obvious if Smith immediately grasped what Terry was really saying. He began explaining why he had named his organization after Frederick Douglass rather than Washington, telling a story about the great antislavery campaigner writing a letter forgiving his former slave master. Terry, in response, asked why the master needed forgiveness at all. Why should he apologize "for giving [Douglass] shelter, food all those years?" Terry asked.

Smith tried to answer—"Let me address the first question"— but he was drowned out by an eruption from the audience. Some laughed, as if they thought Terry was joking. Someone else clapped. Terry continued, muttering, "Why can't we just have segregation?" to no one in particular. Eventually, a CPAC moderator had to step in to restore order.

After things settled down, I raced over to Terry. He was sitting next to a friend, named Matthew Heimbach, who wore a Confederate flag T-shirt (years later, Heimbach would play a major role in organizing the infamous 2017 white supremacist rally in Charlottesville). In our conversation, Terry was very open about what he believed: whites should perpetually control the political system, and Blacks should be locked in a subservient apartheid-like system forever. If Black people don't like it, he said, they "should be allowed to vote in Africa."

That wasn't the part of the conversation that struck me most forcefully, though. There was one thing—an aside, really—that I kept thinking about for years: Terry claimed to be a direct descendant of Confederate president Jefferson Davis. If this was true, it would mean we were related.

My father's family has been in the United States for a very long time. One genealogist traced the Beauchamp clan's lineage back to before the American founding. Davis, the first and only Confederate president, is part of this extended family on my grandmother's side. My great-grandmother, a Davis herself, would often speak of him visiting her childhood house. This lineage makes Davis a distant cousin of mine.

But while Terry celebrated this heritage, I took pride in my father's revolt against it. In high school, my dad would leave his Dallas home on Sunday mornings, telling his father—a city councilor—that he was going to their church. He was actually attending Black churches and staging sit-ins at lunch counters. As a college student at Southern Methodist University, he founded a fraternity that challenged segregation on campus. And as an adult, he married my mother—the daughter of two Holocaust survivors who'd been admitted to the country as refugees—and converted to Judaism.

Growing up hearing this family history turned me into America's littlest patriot. As a child, I took immense pride in my country's defeat of the Confederacy and of Nazi Germany—systems that represented, on each side, my family's shame and its oppression. While in grade school, I read an eight-hundred-page history of World War II at recess. In my favorite computer game, *Civilization II*, I played and replayed scenarios where you could assume leadership of the Union and of the Allied forces—waging just war over and over again, always on the easiest setting to ensure that the right side won.

This was a way of engaging with the history of the United States—celebrating the country's righteous wars and ignoring the many evils it had perpetrated—that grew out of being an upper-middle-class white kid in the idyllic end-of-history 1990s. Unlike for my grandparents who survived death camps, my safety was never seriously at risk. Once, some rowdy kids in my heavily Catholic neighborhood in the DC suburbs knocked over the mailboxes outside the area's Jewish homes. Their parents made the kids apologize and repair them.

But at the same time, my flight to historical comfort emerged from a deeper existential concern. My maternal grandfather, who lived with us for some time, was jumpy and paranoid, his soul scarred by his experiences at Auschwitz. I wondered why my father had to sneak out to attend protests, and how my paternal grandparents—so kind to me when we visited them in Dallas—were seemingly okay with something as monstrous as segregation. My young life was clearly secure and stable, but I had a sense that it might not always be this way: that the easy calm that prevailed in the 1990s was not the permanent order of things, either in the United States or around the world. I came to see democracy as something precious—and to worry that even a society seemingly committed to egalitarian ideals could collapse into something darker.

Scott Terry brought these fears to the fore. He was living proof that a blood relative could look at our shared story and find pride where I found shame, resentment over the history in which I took comfort. In this, he opened my mind to the possibility that the consensus around the basic principles of liberal democracy in countries like the United States might not be nearly as widely shared as it seemed.

IN THE NEXT ten years of my career as a journalist, I watched that possibility become reality. Around the world, powerful political factions in established democracies worked to alter the very fabric of the democratic system, preserving the form of elections while undermining their fairness. When they succeeded, they were able to replace democracy with something altogether different: a system that appeared democratic at first glance but was fundamentally rigged in favor of the ruling party. Political scientists Steven Levitsky and Lucan Way call this system "competitive authoritarianism." It maintains formal democratic rules but breaks those rules "so often and to such an extent . . . that the regime fails to meet conventional minimum standards for democracy." Its operatives gerrymander, rig campaign-finance rules, control the media, politicize the justice system, and harass opposition parties—all quietly enough to maintain the veneer of democracy, but effectively enough to rig elections in their favor.

Competitive authoritarianism is now a common form of government around the globe, often rising at democracy's expense. Perhaps most strikingly, it has even managed to threaten some of the world's most historically stable democracies. Countries where democracy had seemed solidly established for decades, even centuries, have recently seen surges in support for political movements aiming to build a competitive authoritarian regime. The list includes the world's most powerful and influential country (the United States), the most populous nation on the planet (India), large democracies in Latin America (Brazil) and Southeast Asia (the Philippines), the Middle East's only long-standing democracies (Israel and Turkey), and at least two members of the European Union (Hungary and Poland).

Developments in these countries pose a series of puzzles. What is driving the rise of antidemocratic factions inside previously secure democracies? Why is it that these challenges are mostly, albeit not exclusively, coming from the far right? Why are these forces seeking to create competitive authoritarian governments rather than more nakedly antidemocratic fascist or military regimes? And is the current wave of democratic erosion a passing trend or an enduring struggle that will define the future of our planet?

For the past ten years, I've reported from the front lines of the global struggle for democracy—and I've learned that the roots of democracy's global crisis go deeper than almost anyone appreciates.

What's occurring today is not primarily a story about a handful of powerful people; to focus too much on them, even outsized ones like Donald Trump, misses the structural forces that give them power in the first place. To make sense of what was happening, I needed to go beyond the traditional tools of journalism and draw on more scholarly resources: records unearthed by historians, data analyses from political scientists, and foundational debates between philosophers and political theorists over the meaning of "democracy." When I looked at the world through these varied lenses, I saw a deep pattern—not just similarities between antidemocratic factions in different countries today, but a recurring war over democracy that's been waged intermittently for generations. We are living through the latest iteration of this long-running struggle; its outcome is by no means certain.

Scott Terry made this dynamic achingly clear. While few of today's authoritarians share his naked nostalgia for slavery and segregation, his most basic premise—that the world's moves toward social equality have gone too far and need to be rolled back—is the beating heart of antidemocratic politics around the world today. It is a backlash animated by what I've come to call the reactionary spirit: the idea that if democracy threatens existing social hierarchies, it is right and maybe even righteous to overthrow democracy rather than permit social change. The reactionary spirit has haunted democracy for its entire modern existence; today, it is powering an extinction-level threat to its future. To understand this twenty-first-century crisis, we need to start by understanding the reactionary spirit.

CHAPTER 1

WHAT IS THE REACTIONARY SPIRIT?

Democracy, by its nature, encourages the upending of social hierarchies. In authoritarian systems, social elites can protect their status by simply preventing anyone who would challenge them from holding power. In democracies, by contrast, it's always possible for citizens to elect leaders whose policies would challenge the existing social order. One version of such a challenge threatens inequalities of wealth by proposing redistribution of wealth through policies like higher taxes and greater spending on the poor. Another threatens inequalities of status through calls to extend legal rights to marginalized minority groups. Typically, material and social inequalities are deeply connected: when egalitarian forces win power in elections, they often push to level both the economic and the social playing fields.

It's easy to think of historical examples. The rise of Abraham Lincoln and his antislavery Republican Party threatened both the Southern elite's ability to profit from slavery and an entire social order built around slavery, one that many whites saw as the foundation of the Southern way of life. The nineteenth-century Reform Acts in the United Kingdom gradually loosened restrictions on voting and eliminated bogus districts that had almost no electors, ultimately overturning the aristocratic stranglehold on the political system. India's 1949 secular constitution, paired with affirmative action policies for lower castes, aimed to both improve the lot of India's poorest and challenge upper-caste Hindus' privileged social position.

Democracy does not merely enable efforts to change social hierarchies: it actually makes them inevitable. Democratic institutions both create legal avenues for members of oppressed groups to act against their own oppression, and encourage the spread of political ideas that fuel such challenges.

Democracy's core principle is that no person is inherently better than any other; for that reason, we all deserve an equal say in determining how we're governed. Democratic governments preach this idea, in schools and public documents, as the foundation of their own legitimacy. The predictable result is that a significant percentage of citizens come to believe such notions, and thus turn against social and legal inequalities at odds with them. It is difficult to square restrictions on the franchise, extreme economic inequality, or formalized racial discrimination with democracy's most basic egalitarian principle. Every democracy, no matter how unequal at its founding, contains the seeds of its own improvement.

When Frederick Douglass predicted in 1852 that "the doom of slavery is certain," he had this general dynamic in mind. Douglass believed firmly that the Constitution was an antislavery document, that its lofty declarations of equality and human rights were so manifestly at odds with the realities of chattel slavery that the two could not coexist indefinitely. The Constitution's protections of individual rights, including its requirement that every state maintain "a Republican Form of Government," created a solid legal foundation and irresistible moral push toward abolition.

"Slavery is essentially barbarous in its character. It, above all things else, dreads the presence of an advanced civilization. It flourishes best where it meets no reproving frowns, and hears no condemning voices. While in the Union it will meet with both," Douglass argued in an 1860 address to an antislavery meeting in Scotland.

In that same speech, Douglass argued that the South's leaders were fully aware of this reality: "I have much confidence in the instincts of the slaveholders," he noted archly. In order to protect the planter class's tyrannical rule over Blacks, Douglass predicted, the South would choose to abandon American democracy: "Its hope of life, in the last resort, is to get out of the Union." In this, he was not merely prescient; he was putting his finger on the fundamental nature of the reactionary spirit.

Democracy's egalitarian heart poses a perennial problem for those committed, for one reason or another, to preserving inequality. Perhaps they believe in hierarchy as a matter of moral principle, seeing monarchy or women's disenfranchisement as an expression of the natural order. Perhaps they benefit personally from the existing distribution of power and wealth. Often, as in the case of wealthy slaveowners, it's some mix of both.

Regardless, the inevitable tendency of democracy toward political challenge to inequality forces the partisans of hierarchy to make a choice. They can accommodate democracy, attempting to block change through electoral means and reconciling themselves to the real possibility that they might lose. Alternatively, they can choose hierarchy *over* democracy, trying to constrain or even topple democracy to protect hierarchies of wealth and status.

The impulse to make the latter choice is the reactionary spirit. It is a fundamental feature of modern democratic life; it has always been there as democracy does its work to promote social change.

The reactionary spirit is not a specific political movement or tradition, traceable to one geographic place or body of writings. Nor is it simply a term for the political right, or even for right-wing authoritarianism. It is a specific kind of antidemocratic politics that emerges in a country that has democratic institutions, like elections and parliaments, in reaction to the operation of those institutions. The reactionary spirit sees democracy as so threatening to the existing social order that it must be weakened or even abolished entirely. The result is a politics that uses political power in all its forms, ranging from legislation to coups to revolutions, to undermine democracy or overthrow it outright.

"Reaction is not reflex," the political theorist Corey Robin wrote in his book *The Reactionary Mind*. "It begins from a position of principle—that some are fit, and thus ought, to rule others—and then recalibrates that principle in light of a democratic challenge from below."

The post–Civil War South, in both its violent resistance to Reconstruction and the subsequent rise of Jim Crow, offers a striking example of the reactionary spirit at work in America. In response to abolition and Black enfranchisement, Southern states built what the political scientist Robert Mickey calls "authoritarian enclaves" inside a nationally democratic context to ensure that Blacks and their white Republican supporters could never oust local Democratic parties committed to white supremacy.

Internationally, many examples of the reactionary spirit can be found in nineteenth- and twentieth-century Europe. During this era, democracy was struggling to be born, emerging in societies that had long been dominated by absolute monarchs and landed nobility. The spread of elections and legislatures posed an obvious threat to this feudal order, as vesting significant power in parliaments rather than kings would fatally undermine its foundations. Instead of acceding to democratic change, defenders of Europe's ancien régimes used a combination of violence and legal restrictions to arrest democracy's rise. The result, in leading European countries like Germany and France, was a tumultuous and uneven process of democratization—one in which new democratic governments were not infrequently overthrown and replaced by authoritarian forces.

In his study of this time period, Harvard scholar Daniel Ziblatt uncovered an intriguing difference between these countries and others, like Britain and Belgium, that experienced a relatively calm and straightforward pathway to democracy: the countries that did better had stronger and more established conservative political parties.

On its face, this seems counterintuitive—wouldn't a more organized right-wing party make it easier for reactionary forces to undermine democracy? Ziblatt found that the existence of strong conservative parties tended to convince those who might otherwise oppose democracy that they could play by its rules and win. A well-functioning conservative party works, in effect, to reconcile the broader right to democracy—to tame the reactionary spirit.

"Well-organized and highly institutionalized partisan old regime interests provided a way of 'lowering the costs of toleration,' and thus making democracy safe for key segments of old regime elites," Ziblatt wrote. "Conversely, the absence of a well-organized and highly institutionalized party created to effectively defend the most recalcitrant old regime interests made democracy more difficult to construct and less settled and enduring."

Ziblatt's analysis illustrates that the reactionary spirit's emergence as a serious threat to democracy is not an inevitable by-product of social change. Although hierarchies unavoidably have their hardline defenders, they do not always appear as an equal and opposite force to democracy's supporters. The reactionary spirit's rise as a potent political force requires at least one of two things: either a mass bottom-up revolt against change, or an organized faction capable of stoking a wider reactionary panic. You can think of this in supply-and-demand terms: the reactionary spirit is at its strongest when there's both a high demand for reactionary politics and a skilled, well-funded political organization willing to supply it.

It is important to distinguish between reactionary politics in the antidemocratic sense and the political right in general. While conservatives typically see virtue in tradition and danger in change, this does not always and necessarily push them toward authoritarianism. In healthy modern democracies like Canada and Japan, right-wing parties are integrated parts of the democratic landscape; their rule poses no threat to democracy itself. A democratic right understands its core purposes as opposing misguided attempts at social change and enacting reforms that strengthen what's valuable about the existing political order. Some analysts on the left elide this distinction: Robin, for example, argues that "historically, the conservative has sought to stall the march of democracy." But equating conservatism and reaction makes it difficult to understand the many right-wing parties that have operated comfortably within democracy's boundaries.

The reactionary spirit can be distinguished from other forms of conservative politics, even extreme-right politics, in two important ways. First, it arises in reaction to democratic change—either the creation of democratic institutions through revolution or reform, or social change pursued through constitutional means. Something like the 1979 Islamic Revolution in Iran, while undoubtedly both socially conservative and antidemocratic, overthrew a monarchy and thus does not qualify.

Second, the reactionary spirit produces a particular form of extreme-right politics, specifically, an antidemocratic one. This is why the current surge in support for European far-right parties is only partially an expression of the reactionary spirit. Generally, these parties are growing in reaction to a kind of social change that challenges the traditional European social order—mass nonwhite immigration—and have adopted fairly extreme views on the matter. But not all have gone so far as to become enemies of democracy. Many have accepted electoral defeat; some have not even seriously attempted to undermine democracy while in power. As objectionable as these parties' platforms may be to liberals and leftists, it is important for the sake of both analytic clarity and intellectual honesty not to equate even extreme right-wing policy views with hostility to democracy itself.

To clarify what it looks like when the reactionary spirit is actually at work, and how it has become one of the central forces shaping our world today, this book focuses on four examples: the United States, Hungary, Israel, and India. In each of these countries, a conservative party in a seemingly stable democracy has become a vehicle for the ambitions of a far-right strongman bent on locking his political opponents out of power. In each of these countries, that party has undermined basic principles of democracy through measures like changing election rules, politicizing the judiciary, attacking independent media, and abusing regulatory powers for political advantage. And in each of these countries, fears about threats to the existing social hierarchy have been central drivers of the autocratic faction's political success.

These four countries are not only clear examples of the reactionary spirit at work, but influential ones. Together, they have played a uniquely important role in creating a global climate where the reactionary spirit is more powerful than at any point since World War II. Studying them will help us understand both why the reactionary spirit is on the rise at roughly the same time in relatively different countries and why modern reactionaries typically aim to maintain the fiction of democratic elections rather than abolishing them entirely.

THE AMERICANIZATION OF AUTOCRACY

Donald Trump did not attempt to overthrow the 2020 election by asserting a Caesarist right to rule. Instead, he claimed that Biden and the Democrats had, through some improbable conspiracy, managed to rig the count in their favor. Trump and his allies appealed to the rhetoric of democratic fairness with slogans like "Stop the steal," and people believed them. In testimony to the January 6 Committee of the US House of Representatives, multiple participants in the Capitol riot told investigators that their actions were motivated by the idea that a great antidemocratic fraud was being perpetrated upon the American people.

Reactionary leaders in other countries often take a similar line. In Hungary, Prime Minister Viktor Orbán has argued that "there is an absence of democracy . . . in Western Europe" and that his government is pioneering a model of "Christian democracy" to correct it. In Israel, Prime Minister Benjamin Netanyahu described his goal as "the strengthening of democracy." Indian prime minister Narendra Modi is fond of referring to his country as "the mother of democracy," claiming that his government "is continuously strengthening these ancient ideals."

In both the United States and around the world, we have entered a strange era of autocracy without autocrats—where democracies are under assault from within by leaders who claim to be democracy's greatest champions. To contemporary ears, this sounds like simple public relations: everyone agrees that democracy is the best system of government and equates standing for democracy with being on the side of the right and the good. But, historically speaking, reactionaries more typically wore their opposition to democracy on their sleeve, claiming that their preferred authoritarian system was superior to the chaotic and weak democratic alternatives.

Joseph de Maistre, the French-Italian philosopher and statesman, argued after the French Revolution that "a large and free nation cannot exist under a republican government." Otto von Bismarck, the architect of Germany's unification under the kaiser's monarchical rule, declared in 1850, "I see the source of Prussian honor in Prussia keeping her distance from any shameful ties to democracy." Benito Mussolini wrote in 1932 that "fascism trains its guns on the whole block of democratic ideologies, and rejects both their premises and their practical applications. . . . It asserts the irremediable and fertile and beneficent inequality of men who cannot be leveled by any such mechanical and extrinsic device as universal suffrage."

The degree to which authoritarian parties feel the need to take on a democratic guise generally reflects the political and ideological strength of democracy in their country. You can see this quite visibly in pre–World War I Europe, where the aristocracy in different countries took very different approaches to the use of democratic rhetoric. "Where its [the aristocracy's] power is still comparatively unrestricted, as in Germany, it appeals exclusively to the grace of God. But when, as in Italy, it feels insecure, it adds to the appeal to the deity an appeal to the popular will," the sociologist Robert Michels observed in 1911.

Tellingly, there is one place where reactionary movements have always employed the language of democracy and freedom in the way they do today: the United States of America. Understanding the roots of this malign American exceptionalism will show just how much the strategic choices of reactionaries reflect deeper ideological and political realities—and hence clarify why their contemporary leaders around the world don a democratic mask.

The notion of an American authoritarian tradition may sound strange. This is a country widely considered to be the world's oldest continuous democracy; its Constitution, in force since 1789, developed an electoral and political system that has been modified but never fully overhauled. Reverence for the founding and its democratic principles has long been a starting point in mainstream American political discourse, with arguments taking place not over the desirability of democracy but rather over which faction best embodies democracy's core ideals.

Everyone at this point knows the ways in which the United States has fallen short of its principles. Typically, these failures get slotted into one of two ideological narratives: either one of aberrations giving way to a more perfect union, or one of an irredeemable country whose claim to high-minded ideals has always been a vicious sham. Yet there is a third, halfway option. It posits that America is not defined by a single overarching political tradition, but rather by at least two—the first an authentically democratic one, the second authentically authoritarian. These warring traditions, born out of contradictions evident at the founding, have always battled over the country's identity, with each emerging triumphant at different points in time.

The American authoritarian tradition claims, in the apt words of historian Jefferson Cowie, a "right to practice tyranny in the name of the universal philosophical category—freedom." American authoritarianism perverts the language of democracy and rights, advancing a version of these ideas that justifies excluding entire classes of persons from the body politic and ruling over them by force. American reactionaries did not present their ideologies as the negation of democracy, as many of their European peers did. Instead, they described themselves as its greatest defenders.

In a speech to the US Senate in 1861 announcing his resignation, Senator Jefferson Davis explained his defection to the Confederacy as a decision consistent with the "great principles" of American democracy: "that there was no divine right to rule; that no man inherited the right to govern; that there were no classes by which power and place descended to families, but that all stations were equally within the grasp of each member of the body-politic." Davis's paean to democratic values was, of course, entirely at odds with the chattel slavery that his new government stood for. The possession of entire Black families—held by their white owners for generations, abused and separated at the owners' whims—is practically the definition of an inherited class system in which "power and place descended to families."

Yet for my ancestor, it was self-evident that Black people were not equal human beings who deserved to participate in American society. He went even further: it was not slavery that constituted antidemocratic oppression but rather Northern support for abolishing it, a threat so serious that it justified secession.

"We recur to the principles upon which our Government was founded; and when you deny them, and when you deny to us the right to withdraw from a Government which thus perverted threatens to be destructive of our rights, we but tread in the path of our fathers when we proclaim our independence," he said. "This is done not in hostility to others, not to injure any section of the country, not even for our own pecuniary benefit; but from the high and solemn motive of defending and protecting the rights we inherited, and which it is our sacred duty to transmit unshorn to our children."

Similar arguments for authoritarian practices echo throughout American history, be they property qualifications for voting or extreme gerrymandering. This particular antidemocratic politics grew, as Cowie observes, out of America being "founded on a premise so deeply wedded to the combined ancient republican values of freedom and democratic governance." Because democratic values are so essential to what it means to be an American, only the most marginal reactionaries openly rejected them. Effective reactionaries adopted democratic language out of either expedience or sincere conviction. The most successful reactionaries, the ones who won and kept power, built autocratic political systems that retained a democratic veneer—pioneering competitive authoritarianism because the American democratic ideology left them no other choice.

Competitive authoritarianism has spread globally in the late twentieth and early twenty-first centuries in large part because global politics has become more ideologically American. The cataclysm of World War II discredited the overt European reactionary tradition, linking naked hostility to rights and democracy with the horrors of Nazism. The democratic ideals European reactionaries had rejected for so long became the foundation of the postwar Atlantic political order—and, more broadly, an essential part of both the Western struggle against communism and colonized people's struggles against Western empires. The international system created by the Allies after 1945 is widely referred to as the "liberal international order" for a reason: it was built around an at least rhetorical commitment to translating liberal political ideals into principles that governed political life for the whole of the human race.

The United Nations Universal Declaration of Human Rights, adopted by the UN General Assembly in 1948 without a single dissenting vote, was explicit on this point. "Everyone has the right to take part in the government of his country, directly or through freely chosen representatives," it announced. "The will of the people shall be the basis of the authority of government; this will shall be expressed in periodic and genuine elections which shall be by universal and equal suffrage and shall be held by secret vote or by equivalent free voting procedures."

Once again, real-world politics were at odds with the lofty rhetoric: even the increasingly democratic West supported all sorts of antidemocratic regimes in the name of fighting communism. But the process of global Americanization, of democracy coming to occupy the same hegemonic ideological position that it long had in the United States, continued nonetheless. It reached its apogee after the fall of the Soviet Union in 1991, when there truly was no longer any plausible alternative to democracy. Dozens of nondemocratic governments remained in power, but their political models had little global appeal. Increasingly, democracy became the ideal to which people everywhere aspired.

This constituted a revolution in world politics—and an astonishingly fast one. According to V-Dem, the leading academic database on democracy, only 8 percent of countries worldwide were democracies in 1945. Sixty years later, that figure had increased to 52 percent. That sixty-year period was a time not just when outright authoritarian governments fell, but when democracies themselves became substantially more democratic. By the end of the twentieth century, restrictions on the franchise based on gender and race had been widely abolished. Once-unthinkable moves toward social equality, like women winning national elections, became reality. Colonial empires collapsed, with millions of former subjects becoming citizens either in their new countries or (via immigration) in the European states that had once oppressed them.

Such rapid social change was bound to inflame the reactionary spirit, and indeed it did. This is why it seems that so many established democracies are in crisis at the same time: all of them, to one degree or another, experienced radical and successful challenges to traditional social hierarchies in the late twentieth and early twenty-first centuries. What seem like disparate events—the post-1947 development of Indian secularism, the 1990s Oslo Accords between Israel and the

Palestinians, the 2008 election of Barack Obama, the EU's relatively open-borders response to the 2015 refugee crisis—were all part of this general move toward a more egalitarian world. And each of them galvanized significant reactionary resistance.

But the ideological parameters of global politics had shifted permanently. Stark reactionary denunciations of democracy of the sort once offered by Mussolini could no longer command majority support in established democracies. To adapt, antidemocratic factions around the world have started acting like their American peers always had: using democratic language, competing in elections, and then hollowing out democracy from within once in power.

These foreign movements do not typically copy American ones. It's more like what biologists call "convergent evolution," in which different species with no direct contact or shared ancestors evolve similar traits under similar environmental pressures. Much like how North American hedgehogs and Australian echidnas both evolved spines to ward off predators, reactionary leaders around the world have adopted competitive authoritarianism in response to domestic political environments where overtly opposing democracy is prohibitively unpopular. Faced with similar circumstances, they arrived at the same approach: portraying themselves as democracy's truest defenders while actually undermining it.

Understanding the current crisis of democracy in these terms helps explain some puzzles about the current wave of antidemocratic politics—for which many diagnoses have been offered, none of which are fully persuasive. One popular theory suggests that our era is one of competition between democratic states and openly authoritarian ones. President Joe Biden, for example, has repeatedly argued that the twenty-first century will be determined by America's ability to prove that democracy works better than the Russian or especially Chinese authoritarian model. This could eventually turn out to be true: historically, perceptions of a political system's ability to deliver tangible results really do affect its survival prospects.

However, there is little evidence today that Chinese state capitalism—let alone the weakened post-Ukraine-invasion Russian dictatorship—is seen as more likely to deliver than democracy. Inside long-standing democracies, where the most dangerous cases of democratic decline can be found, there are no viable parties vowing to bring China's system to their countries the way fascist and communist factions once credibly contested elections. China and Russia have played very limited direct roles in the rise of reactionary political movements in established democracies, having little to do with the extremist turn of factions like Likud in Israel and the Bharatiya Janata Party (BJP) in India. The most high-profile attempt to encourage democratic crisis abroad, Russia's meddling in the 2016 US election, appears to have been largely ineffectual. Dictatorships are not responsible for the current democratic crisis.

A second explanation is rising economic inequality: that the people left behind by the modern globalized economy are frustrated and angry, so much so that they lash out at minority groups and even democracy itself. This theory is popular on both the far right, as it turns partisans of reactionary movements into victims rather than oppressors, and on the socialist left, as it assimilates novel developments into a familiar class-based narrative. But the theory is Western-centric, only making sense in advanced economies whose working class has suffered from deindustrialization. India is among globalization's biggest winners, and both Israel and Hungary have grown much richer over the past three decades. Moreover, the narrative's "working-class revolt" premise is likely false even in the West: statistical research on Europe and the United States generally shows that class does a poor job of explaining why people tend to support antidemocratic and far-right factions. It is members of groups with high social status—some wealthy, some not—that are most likely to back antidemocratic movements, reflecting rising challenges to the social hierarchy that has long benefited them.

This is not to say that inequality is irrelevant to the rise of the reactionary spirit. In fact, it's crucial. The global superrich have allied with authoritarian factions to protect their financial interests from the left's plans for redistribution, providing the far right with critical funding and resources. But this is an elite-level story, not a mass public one. It does not vindicate the idea that *popular* support for antidemocratic politics today comes from rage at an unjust economic order, a notion that is generally not supported by the evidence.

Finally, and relatedly, there's a theory that "populism" in general is responsible for democratic backsliding. Populism is typically defined as a political style that pits a virtuous public against a corrupt elite, calling on the people to retake control of a system managed by a narrow set of selfish or out-of-touch interests. And indeed, reactionary leaders like Trump and Netanyahu regularly employ populist rhetoric.

But this theory confuses symptom with cause. It's true that antidemocratic politicians often employ a populist rhetoric style, but so do ones that operate inside democratic boundaries. Many left-wing populist leaders, like Bernie Sanders, or parties, like Greece's Syriza, have achieved significant influence in their countries but have done little that could plausibly be seen as threatening the foundations of the democratic system. Populism on its own is not the problem; the danger arises when populism gets deployed for authoritarian ends. And at present, these dynamics are concentrated on the right side of the aisle.

There's nothing about left-wing politics that makes it immune to the authoritarian temptation, as the historical examples of Stalin, Mao, and the Khmer Rouge show. This left-wing authoritarian tradition is alive and well today, particularly in Latin America. But in the kinds of countries we're studying—well-established democracies that have slid toward competitive authoritarianism—the political parties responsible have overwhelmingly been on the right. Any explanation for what's happening today needs to take into account the strong right-wing tilt of contemporary authoritarian politics in established democracies—a fact better explained by the theory of the reactionary spirit than by a critique of populism in general.

I want to emphasize, again, that not all right-wing politics is antidemocratic. The reactionary spirit is something more specific: a curdling of conservatism into a willingness to engage in scorched-earth politics, to assail the democratic system itself in order to prevent it from transforming the country in a more egalitarian direction. This is not "normal" right-wing politics, of the sort that Ziblatt diagnosed as essential for democracy to flourish. Instead, it is what happens when the conventional right gets overtaken by its reactionary rivals.

The situation is epitomized by the United States, where conservative judge J. Michael Luttig lamented in 2023 that "there is no Republican Party" anymore, only a reactionary organization that bears its name. But this outmuscling is happening on a global scale—and now threatens to collectively undo the democratic victories of the post–World War II era.

WHAT IS DEMOCRACY ANYWAY?

There's one more thing I need to clarify early on: what I mean when I talk about democracy.

The political scientist Adam Przeworski defines democracy as "a political regime in which rulers are selected through free and contested elections. Operationally, democracy is a regime in which incumbents lose elections and leave office if they do." This definition is useful because it sets up a simple binary test for when a country is and isn't a democracy—and, in doing so, clarifies how a system can be authoritarian while still holding elections. If there are regular contests, but they're not held under free conditions and don't oust incumbents, then it's not a democracy by Przeworski's definition. Contemporary Hungary, where Orbán's party has won the last four national elections in a row and currently controls about 90 percent of all media in the country, is an example of a country that pretends to be a democracy but obviously isn't.

Yet Przeworski's definition depends on a vague word—"free"—that demands explanation. What does it mean for an election to be held under free conditions? And how do we know if and when an election qualifies? This is where a deeper understanding of democracy comes into play—one that centers on democracy's core value of equality.

Born in reaction to absolute monarchy, modern democracy's most basic principle is that no one person deserves more of a say in setting society's rules than anyone else. Elections are merely a mechanism used to turn this ideal of government by the people into reality, giving everyone as equal a say as possible in choosing their leaders. Obviously, people will disagree about which candidates should win. But as long as the process is fair, voters still believe that they have to respect the outcome because they—and all their fellow citizens—had a roughly equal say in the outcome.

Elizabeth Anderson, a political philosopher at the University of Michigan, has aptly defined democracy with the value of equality in mind. She described it as "collective self-determination by means of open discussion among equals, in accordance with rules acceptable to all. To stand as an equal before others in discussion means that one is entitled to participate, that others recognize an obligation to listen respectfully and respond to one's arguments, that no one need bow and scrape before others or represent themselves as inferior to others as a condition of having their claim heard."

When we talk about an election being "free," or "free and fair," we talk about it taking place under conditions that approximate the ones Anderson describes: where all citizens get to vote and campaign for their preferred candidates, under equitable rules, without anyone in the government or otherwise wielding power and privilege to cheat the system.

Obviously, the Andersonian ideal isn't fully borne out in reality. Even in the world's most egalitarian democracies, certain wealthy and influential people wield far more influence over the political process than the average citizen. Part of the task of democratic politics is to recognize and curtail the distorting influence of these inequalities as much as possible, working to make it harder and harder for the powerful to unfairly dominate everyone else. There's plenty of room for reasonable disagreement about the policies that best promote fair and equal access to the political system; different democracies take different approaches, and that's totally appropriate.

But while no democracy is perfect, there's still a bright line between even a deeply flawed democratic system like the one in the contemporary United States and an outright authoritarian one like Hungary's. Though both have political processes marred by inequalities of wealth and power, the United States still has free and fair national elections in which either major party can win. Robust protections are in place for free speech and freedom of assembly; the media is not owned by the ruling party and airs a diverse range of opinions. The situation in the United States is worrying not because it has already become Hungary, but because it is taking on certain Hungarian traits. America has been backsliding away from democracy but has not yet fallen into the competitive authoritarian abyss.

The American and Hungarian cases help us see that democracy is both a binary *and* a spectrum. It's true that some countries are democracies while others are not, and it's important to keep that bright line in mind. It's also true that some democracies are more democratic than others, even if they all meet the minimum standards that separate them from autocracy. Of the four countries this book focuses on, only one—Hungary—has fully crossed the authoritarian threshold. The other three—the United States, Israel, and India—remain on the democratic side of the line but have recently been moving in the wrong direction.

To fully grasp how the reactionary spirit degrades democracy, we need to keep Anderson's definition of democracy in mind: it is really about creating a society where citizens are each other's political equals. A country that holds elections, even competitive ones, can still backslide away from democracy if it attacks political equality in other ways. Restrictions on the press, crackdowns on civil rights groups, politicization of courts and law enforcement, repression of ethnic or religious minorities—these are all examples of ways that democracy can be eroded without frontal assaults on elections like ballot stuffing.

Some say that such concerns are not, properly speaking, about democracy at all. Rights protecting free speech and minorities are instead described as "liberal" rights, using the term not in the partisan American sense but in the philosophical one.

Liberalism as a political philosophy is primarily concerned with rights and freedoms, seeing the task of government as securing individuals' ability to live in a manner of their own choosing. Democracy is, for liberals, the only system of government that extends this idea of self-determination to the political realm—granting people the right to choose, as a collective, how they want their society to be governed. The modern history of democracy is deeply bound up with liberalism: it's not an exaggeration to say democracy as we know it grew out of the work of liberal philosophers, liberal politicians, and liberal political movements.

Despite this interconnection, conceptual tension exists between liberalism and democracy. There are plenty of historical examples of duly elected representatives passing laws that restrict individual rights, and plenty of examples of liberals concluding that it would be right for an unelected institution, like a high court, to overturn those laws. This problem—that majorities sometimes pass illiberal laws, and the legal remedy for them is often undemocratic—has been termed the "counter-majoritarian difficulty." It's a thorny theoretical dilemma with practical implications for all sorts of major policy areas.

But at the same time, not every legal restriction on individual rights is an example of a conflict between liberalism and democracy. Certain rights are so fundamental to democratic equality that no system can be considered truly democratic without them. When the press is muzzled, when millions are enslaved, when entire minority groups are forbidden from participating in the political system or making their case to the majority, fundamental democratic principles are violated. All people are not being treated as equals entitled to participate in political life on a level playing field. Such cases are not examples of tension between liberalism and democracy; they are examples of breaks with basic *democratic* principles. Even a government backed by a majority cannot justly crush press freedom or restrict the franchise to particular ethnic groups, because doing so would attack the foundation of democratic legitimacy: public consent via free and fair elections. It's not democratic to pass laws designed to ensure that you stay in power forever.

The relationship between liberalism and democracy will come up frequently in this book, in part because reactionary thinkers and politicians take advantage of it to paint their project in a more sympathetic light. Throughout American history, advocates of racial hierarchy often described themselves as standing up for liberal rights and freedoms against a tyrannical majority—much as Jefferson Davis did in his Senate speech defending the Confederacy. Today's reactionaries often flip the script, claiming to defend democracy against liberals who are imposing radical values on a culturally conservative majority. "The situation in the West is that there is liberalism, but there is no democracy," as Viktor Orbán put it in a 2018 speech. "The liberal concept of freedom of opinion has gone so far that liberals see diversity of opinion as important—up until the point that they realize, to their shock, that there are opinions which are different from theirs."

But the reactionary spirit is truthfully neither liberal nor democratic. That it can speak the language of both fluently, twisting liberal and democratic ideals to defend authoritarian political projects, is a testament to just how subtly effective it can be. The reactionary spirit is not mere gut reflex, but rather a sophisticated and enduring political force that has shaped life in wildly different countries at wildly different times.

In our era, it has emerged as the greatest threat to democracy's survival. To address this danger, we must begin by understanding it.

CHAPTER 2

ALL-AMERICAN AUTHORITARIANISM

Three years after I met Scott Terry at CPAC, I attended another major conservative gathering, the 2016 Republican National Convention in Cleveland. While there, I went to a party hosted by one of my contacts, a radical young conservative named Milo Yiannopoulos, who was hosting what he termed a "Gays for Trump" celebration midway through the event.

Milo was a gay British writer with platinum-blond hair and an outsized persona, the sort of person universally referred to by his first name alone. In 2016, he had emerged as one of the star writers at Breitbart, Steve Bannon's website and the premier online outlet for the pro-Trump right. Milo delighted in provocative stunts like declaring his birthday "World Patriarchy Day" or creating a "Yiannopoulos Privilege Grant" scholarship for white men. He wrote favorably about the racist and anti-Semitic alt-right movement, praising its "youthful energy and jarring, taboo-defying rhetoric."

On the morning of the "Gays for Trump" event, Milo had been banned from Twitter for spearheading a harassment campaign against Black actress Leslie Jones. His inflammatory schtick was a perfect fit for the mood of the American right during Trump's ascendancy, a time of raw, seemingly unbounded extremism. He would soon be tapped to deliver a keynote address at CPAC 2017 (ultimately, he was disinvited after comments surfaced in which he seemingly defended pedophilia).

Unlike some other conservatives, he also was all too willing to cooperate with the mainstream media. When I wrote about him, no matter how critically, he'd send me a note of praise and encouragement. After I published a piece accusing him of "mainstreaming naked racism, sexism, and various other forms of bigotry," he emailed me to say, "I thought your analysis was smart." He understood that his success was a product of attention—"The press serves me like it serves Trump," he said in one of our chats—and that talking to journalists was a good way to get more of it. So when I asked him if I could attend his soiree in Cleveland, he was more than happy to send me an invite.

The party was held in a ballroom on the campus of Cleveland State University, its walls adorned with photos of thin, young, topless men wearing "Make America Great Again" hats. The average attendee wore cargo shorts and stayed far away from the dance floor. The VIPs, such as they were, hailed from various corners of the fringe right-wing world. Pamela Geller, an anti-Muslim blogger who had called Barack Obama the "jihadi-in-chief," was there, wearing a rainbow-sequin shirt emblazoned with the slogan "Love Will Win." Roosh V, an American men's-rights blogger of Iranian descent who had bragged about sleeping with overly intoxicated women, was there. So were Geert Wilders, a Dutch member of parliament who opposed all Muslim immigration, and Richard Spencer, the alt-right "intellectual" who had argued for deporting America's Jews to Israel.

In theory, the party aimed to highlight the dangers violent Islamism posed to gay Americans; Geller, Wilders, and Milo all gave speeches on the subject. But as Roosh's and Spencer's attendance suggested, the event was in practice more of a convening space for reactionaries of all stripes. They weren't partying in defiance of ISIS but in celebration of Trump's coronation—proof, in their mind, that their side was winning.

Around two a.m., after the event had wound down, Milo and I were chatting in a nearby parking garage. Clad in a white tank top decorated with a rainbow-sequin gun, he expounded on the nature of the far right's victory in between cigarette puffs.

"My readers are the most unfashionable people in the world . . . and they're the ones who are going to put Trump in office," he said. "We're building a new party. The old party, I hope, dies—it deserves to die."

This new GOP, in his telling, would be a "libertarian" bulwark against the allegedly "authoritarian" left—politically correct censors looking to impose their values on an unwilling country. But wait a second, I said. Donald Trump wants to ban Muslims from immigrating to the United States. That's more than a little bit authoritarian.

"Yeah, sure," he admitted. "But I'm not a blanket libertarian about everything."

A ban on Muslim migration, he said, was about "protecting American women and minorities" from "the influx of Islam and the ugly cultures that come with it." By restructuring US immigration policy on explicitly bigoted lines, Milo argued, Trump would be "reaffirming the principles on which America was founded."

In just one short conversation, Milo had managed to encapsulate the enduring nature of the American reactionary spirit. It is a backlash against social change, in this case immigration, that manifests in support for authoritarian policies, all the while insisting that the reactionaries are defending America's eternal democratic ideals. Contra American mythology, authoritarian enforcement of the social hierarchy is a common feature of our history. Examples include restricting the franchise to propertied men in colonial and post-Revolutionary America, Pinkerton assaults on striking laborers during the Gilded Age, the arrest and torture of suffragettes after a Washington demonstration in 1917, both Red Scares, and the police raid on the Stonewall Inn.

This reactionary repression emerges especially strongly when members of oppressed groups organize to demand equality—a pattern perhaps most clearly seen when Black people are making the demands. The fight for abolition led to secession and the Confederacy. The Reconstruction-era struggle for Black equality led to the rise of Jim Crow and the creation of competitive authoritarian enclaves in Southern states. And the successful twentieth-century struggle for civil rights, a victory symbolized by a Black man's election to the presidency in 2008, gave rise to America's current democratic crisis. "The trigger for white rage, inevitably, is black advancement," Emory University historian Carol Anderson wrote in her book *White Rage*.

In each of these cases, the political pattern was basically the same: a backlash to social change that produced a reactionary assault on democratic norms and institutions. But the specifics of each racial reactionary wave were importantly different. In each case, the reactionary spirit's avatars adopted language and policies that seemed reasonable and even liberal-democratic to many people alive at the time.

By studying the political consequences of struggles over racial equality, we can see the reactionary spirit's operation in America most plainly—and learn more about how it operates around the world today. The history of America's racial conflicts shows how the reactionary spirit has repeatedly flourished in a place where democracy is the dominant ideology. This centuries-old American pattern is, in our time, repeating itself across the globe.

SLAVERY AND THE REVOLUTION'S AUTHORITARIAN TAINT

Alexis de Tocqueville's *Democracy in America*, the first volume of which was published in 1835, is perhaps the most famous account of political life in the young United States. Tocqueville was much impressed by the vitality of the new country's democratic institutions, seeing deep democratic roots in American cultural and social life. European-style aristocracy, according to the French nobleman, could never take root in such a culturally egalitarian country.

"A republican form of government seems to me to be the natural state of the Americans; which nothing but the continued action of hostile causes, always acting in the same direction, could change into a monarchy," Tocqueville wrote. "I cannot imagine that they will ever bestow the exclusive exercise of [political rights] upon a privileged class of citizens, or, in other words, that they will ever found an aristocracy."

Yet he discovered one place where this national democratic culture was far weaker: the South. There, democracy still reigned rhetorically, but it was uncomfortably wed to a feudal social structure.

"I have explained the reasons why it was impossible ever to establish a powerful aristocracy in America; these reasons existed with less force to the south-west of the Hudson," Tocqueville argued. There, wealthy planters long constituted a "superior class" that amounted to a "kind of aristocracy"; their masses of inherited land and property remade their character and worldview into something closer to that of the haughty and hierarchical European nobility.

The key institution shaping this cultural divide, in Tocqueville's mind, was slavery. Slave owning turned the South into a fundamentally different region—one far more hostile to the democratic principle of equality.

"The citizen of the Southern States of the Union is invested with a sort of domestic dictatorship, from his earliest years; the first notion he acquires in life is that he is born to command, and the first habit which he contracts is that of being obeyed without resistance," he wrote. While Northerners had "the characteristic good and evil qualities of the middle classes," Southerners had "the tastes, the prejudices, the weaknesses, and the magnanimity of all aristocracies."

Tocqueville's observations have been fleshed out by contemporary research. When University of Maryland historian Holly Brewer recently examined the legal and intellectual scaffolding for American slavery, she uncovered a straight line back to feudal English ideas about the authority of monarchs. Carefully tracing the legal arguments and royal proclamations that underpinned the British slave trade, Brewer found that the Stuart kings treated slavery as an extension of an unalterable natural hierarchy of humanity: kings at the top and African slaves at the bottom. Entire families could be bought and sold in perpetuity, on this thinking, because one's place in life was determined by one's blood. "For the Stuarts, race was subsumed within a larger rationale celebrating hereditary status. One was born a slave, just as one was born a prince," Brewer wrote.

The year 1660, when Charles II retook the throne for the Stuarts, proved to be a pivotal year in chattel slavery's American rise. Charles was such a staunch proponent of slavery that he minted coins depicting himself with the elephant and castle symbols of the Royal African Company (RAC), a state-backed corporation tasked with seizing control of the transatlantic slave trade from Dutch competitors. The years following his rise to power saw a series of swift moves toward the institutionalization of chattel slavery in England's colonial holdings.

"Before 1660, colonial laws treated 'servants'—as both whites and blacks were usually called—similarly, if badly," Brewer wrote. "Only with the restoration of hereditary monarchy in 1660 did colonies pass laws enshrining hereditary slavery: Barbados in 1661, Virginia in 1662, Jamaica and Maryland in 1664. These laws were a response to Charles II's explicit requests to his governors to support the RAC."

The origin of chattel slavery in America, per Brewer, is the literal application of authoritarian ideas to a new context. So the American Revolution, premised as it was on the Declaration of Independence's claim that "all men are created equal," created a problem: how could these newly united states reconcile the essentially feudal practice of slavery with Revolutionary liberal-democratic ideals?

The concept of biological race provided America's founders with a makeshift solution. By describing race as a natural reality, they could maintain their rejection of divine-right monarchy while also insisting on the truth of a racial hierarchy partly derived from it. To reconcile slavery and democratic equality, America's founders clothed a feudal ideology in the finery of Enlightenment rationality.

The tension inherent in this position can best be seen in the writing of Thomas Jefferson. Both a slave owner and a leading racial theoretician, Jefferson declared in 1781, "Blacks, whether originally a distinct race, or made distinct by time and circumstances, are inferior to the whites in the endowments both of body and mind." But he also wrote that slavery was a moral atrocity, predicting its downfall in the not-so-distant future. One of his early drafts of the Declaration even included a condemnation of the African slave trade, accusing King George III of attacking the "sacred rights of life & liberty" by enslaving "a distant people who never offended him."

Of all the founders, Jefferson was perhaps the most committed to freedom and democracy in principle; Tocqueville termed him "the most powerful advocate democracy has ever sent forth." The incongruities in his writing on race reflect the undeniable inconsistency between this commitment and his support of slavery. That a man as brilliant as Jefferson could marshal only risible arguments for race as a biological reality—claiming, among other things, that Blacks "secrete less by the kidneys, and more by the glands of the skin"—is not an accident. Rather, it's evidence that the attempt to reconcile democracy and slavery through race was a political maneuver doomed to collapse under the weight of its own contradictions.

"Judging slavery essential to the project of extending the sovereignty of the United States over the American continent, [Jefferson] tried to resolve the contradiction between enslavement and the natural right to freedom by interpreting slavery as a fact of the slaves' inferior nature," historian Barbara Fields wrote. "To that end, he formulated the notion of race, draping its ideological nakedness in a tissue of purported scientific argument so thin that he would surely have seen through it on any subject less central to his nation-founding project than slavery."

Jefferson, like the country he helped create, was torn between two contradictory ideologies: a liberal-democratic gospel of universal human equality, and a feudal-authoritarian vision premised on the idea of fundamental human inequality. As time went on, and the conflict between these strains became clearer, slavery's defenders did away with Jefferson's contortions and boldly asserted the fundamental *inequality* of humankind.

John C. Calhoun was this authoritarian tradition's greatest advocate. A philosopher, wealthy landowner, South Carolina senator, and vice president in two different administrations, he was one of the towering figures in antebellum politics. In 1848, Calhoun summarized the essence of American authoritarianism in a speech attacking the Declaration's (which is to say, Jefferson's) claims about moral equality. Calhoun believed that the idea of political equality depended on the assumption that all people are equally qualified to use freedom responsibly. But this, he claimed, was false: certain people are better and more equipped than others. Those people can and should enjoy a greater degree of liberty than those who could not be so trusted.

"Just in proportion as a people are ignorant, stupid, debased, corrupt, exposed to violence within and danger from without, the power necessary for government to possess, in order to preserve society against anarchy and destruction becomes greater and greater, and individual liberty less and less, until the lowest condition is reached, when absolute and despotic power becomes necessary on the part of the government, and individual liberty extinct," the senator argued.

As obviously undemocratic as a call for the exercise of "absolute and despotic power" may seem, it was the logical extension of Calhoun's broader proslavery position. His speech was primarily concerned with opposing the Oregon Bill, which would recognize Oregon as an official US territory in which slavery was banned. The bit about equality was a response to abolitionists, who cited the Declaration of Independence in favor of their antislavery position. Calhoun's stance, in brief, was not that they were misinterpreting Jefferson but that Jefferson was himself mistaken. All men were not created equal; "to this error, [the] proposition to exclude slavery from the territory northwest of the Ohio may be traced."

Here we see a pure example of the reactionary spirit at work. In the Oregon Bill debate, Calhoun felt obligated to choose between democracy's ideal of equality on the one hand and preserving the slave hierarchy on the other. His response was not only to reject equality, but to advocate antidemocratic ideas—specifically, the use of "absolute and despotic power"— to keep slaves in chains.

Not that Calhoun saw himself as an authoritarian. His stated views on the proper role of the state—"government has no right to control individual liberty beyond what is necessary to the safety and well-being of society"—sounded positively libertarian. To hear Calhoun tell it, it was *abolitionism* that posed a threat to American liberty. Slave ownership, in his mind, was a fundamental right with which the government had no business interfering. Slavery "involves not just our liberty, but what is greater (if to freemen anything can be), existence itself," he said in 1836. "The relation which now exists between the two races in the slaveholding states has existed for two centuries. It has grown with our growth, and strengthened with our strength. It has entered into and modified all our institutions, civil and political. None other can be substituted."

Calhoun here is positioning an authoritarian policy, slavery, as essential to freedom—and any attempt to quash it by a numerical majority as an abuse of power. This is a key rhetorical weapon in the American reactionary arsenal, one that relies on exploiting the counter-majoritarian difficulty by positioning reactionaries as liberalism's champions against majority tyranny. Calhoun's position is specious: there is no human right to own other humans, and thus no dilemma created by elected majorities banning slavery. But in a political context where one could not simply declare that democratic government and ideals should be thrown out entirely, a logical maneuver, or con, was needed to render slavery something other than what it was. Authoritarianism needed to be recast as freedom, true democracy as oppression.

This idea had far-reaching implications for American democracy—especially during the early rise of the abolitionist movement.

In 1831, William Lloyd Garrison launched *The Liberator*, an influential antislavery broadsheet. In 1833, the American Anti-Slavery Society held its first meeting. In 1835, abolitionist organizations around the country launched a massive letter-writing campaign, sending antislavery pamphlets to slave owners in the South and petitions to Congress calling for federal limitations on slavery's expansion to new territories. This was democratic politics through democratic means: urging the overthrow of a hierarchical social system through social organizing and political speech.

Slave owners and their allies were faced with a choice: they could engage with the abolitionists purely on democratic terms or pair their proslavery arguments with blatant undemocratic repression of the antislavery movement. On the main, they chose the latter route—with Southern states persecuting abolitionists and criminalizing abolition advocacy. Missouri, for example, passed a law in 1837 that would "prohibit the publication, circulation, and promulgation of the abolition doctrines," punishable by sentences up to life imprisonment. When forced to choose between slavery and protecting core democratic rights *for whites*, American reactionaries chose the former time and again.

Calhoun was, per usual, the most articulate expositor of proslavery thinking. His greatest fear, according to an 1837 speech, was that the abolitionists would succeed in changing America through the eminently democratic means of changing citizens' minds:

> They who imagine that the spirit now abroad in the North, will die away of itself without a shock or convulsion, have formed a very inadequate conception of its real character; it will continue to rise and spread, unless prompt and efficient measures to stay its progress be adopted. Already it has taken possession of the pulpit, of the schools, and, to a considerable extent, of the press; those great instruments by which the mind of the rising generation will be formed. However sound the great body of the non-slaveholding States are at present, in the course of a few years they will be succeeded by those who will have been taught to hate the people and institutions of nearly one-half of this Union, with a hatred more deadly than one hostile nation ever entertained towards another.

Calhoun's nightmare was that democracy might work. The proper response could not be to meekly accede to the will of the future abolitionist majority; it must instead be to curtail core democratic rights to prevent this majority's emergence.

To some contemporary observers, like future president Abraham Lincoln, the antidemocratic nature of the Southern case for slavery was obvious. "As I would not be a slave, so I would not be a master. This expresses my idea of democracy," he once wrote.

The linkage between slavery and authoritarianism is a persistent theme in Lincoln's thought. In an 1854 speech, he argued that slavery was not only a "monstrous injustice," but one that "deprives our republican example of its just influence in the world—enables the enemies of free institutions, with plausibility, to taunt us as hypocrites—causes the real friends of freedom to doubt our sincerity, and especially because it forces so many really good men amongst ourselves into an open war with the very fundamental principles of civil liberty." Lincoln may have had in mind the famous gibe from the British author Samuel Johnson, issued at the time of the Revolution: "How is it that we hear the loudest yelps for liberty among the drivers of Negroes?"

In 1858, during his seventh and final Senate campaign debate with Senator Stephen Douglas, Lincoln described slavery as the intellectual and legal descendant of absolute monarchy: "No matter in what shape it comes, whether from the mouth of a king who seeks to bestride the people of his own nation and live by the fruit of their labor, or from one race of men as an apology for enslaving another race, it is the same tyrannical principle."

Though such claims were familiar at the time, we are not accustomed to thinking in those terms today. Generally speaking, modern Americans describe slavery as either an alien blight on a generally democratic nation or an expression of the ugly American reality behind that democratic mask. It's clarifying to hear, from perhaps our greatest president, a third option: that slavery represented an authentically American authoritarian ideology, one that has forever struggled for political supremacy with the liberal-democratic project announced in the Declaration of Independence. This ideology is a quintessential American expression of the reactionary spirit—a sense that social hierarchy is not only a reality, but a *good and just* reality. It is a politically potent sentiment, especially when combined with economic self-interest (such as the planter class's desire to maintain fortunes built on the backs of human property).

When that hierarchy of race and wealth came under existential threat, after Lincoln's victory in the 1860 presidential election, it triggered the gravest political crisis in American history.

South Carolina, Calhoun's state, was the first to secede. In its Declaration of Independence, it did not accuse Lincoln of winning power through fraud or other undemocratic means. Instead, it railed against the will of the majority: "A geographical line has been drawn across the Union, and all the States north of that line have united in the election of a man to the high office of President of the United States, whose opinions and purposes are hostile to slavery. . . . The guaranties of the Constitution will then no longer exist; the equal rights of the States will be lost. The slaveholding States will no longer have the power of self-government, or self-protection, and the Federal Government will have become their enemy."

The next year, Confederate vice president Alexander Stephens gave an address expanding on these themes—an address chiefly remembered for its claim that slavery was the "cornerstone" upon which the Confederacy was built. Yet Stephens's argument was even more sweeping: that the Southern cause was not merely a defense of slavery as an institution, but an expression of a deeper philosophical idea behind it. The purpose of the Confederacy, per Stephens, was to create an openly hierarchical America untainted by Jeffersonian ideals of equality:

> The prevailing ideas entertained by [Jefferson] and most of the leading statesmen at the time of the formation of the old constitution, were that the enslavement of the African was in violation of the laws of nature; that it was wrong in principle, socially, morally, and politically. It was an evil they knew not well how to deal with, but the general opinion of the men of that day was that, somehow or other in the order of Providence, the institution would be evanescent and pass away. This idea, though not incorporated in the constitution, was the prevailing idea at that time. The constitution, it is true, secured every essential guarantee to the institution while it should last, and hence no argument can be justly urged against the constitutional guarantees thus secured, because of the common sentiment of the day. Those ideas, however, were fundamentally wrong. They rested upon the assumption of the equality of races. This was an error. It was a sandy foundation, and the government built upon it fell when the "storm came and the wind blew."
>
> Our new government is founded upon exactly the opposite idea; its foundations are laid, its cornerstone rests, upon the great truth that the negro is not equal to the white man; that slavery subordination to the superior race is his natural and normal condition. This, our new government,

is the first, in the history of the world, based upon this great physical, philosophical, and moral truth.

The Confederacy, as a project, was an attempt to resolve the tension between democracy and the authoritarianism of chattel slavery in favor of the latter. That's not how Stephens would have put it. He insisted, in the Cornerstone Speech, that the Confederate constitution "amply secures all our ancient rights, franchises, and liberties." But that was only to show just how well adapted the American reactionary spirit was to its environment.

An entire new country could be founded in the American South on the proposition of inequality and eternal human bondage. Yet this project, so fundamentally feudal in orientation, was seen by its advocates as a defense of freedom and self-government—the beginning of a pattern that American reactionaries would follow for generations to come.

RECONSTRUCTION, JIM CROW, AND THE INVENTION OF COMPETITIVE AUTHORITARIANISM

After the Civil War, the victorious Union government launched the greatest assault on social hierarchy in the young country's history. The postwar constitutional amendments were together meant to resolve the long-running fight between racial authoritarianism and democracy in the latter's favor. The Thirteenth abolished slavery, the Fourteenth guaranteed all citizens "equal protection under the laws," and the Fifteenth prohibited denying a person the vote on grounds of "race, color, or previous condition of servitude." Reconstruction, the Northern effort to rebuild and transform the South after the war, aimed to ensure that these were not mere words on paper; federal officials worked hand in glove with freed Blacks to try to build a new South around the principle of political and racial equality.

This noble effort predictably inflamed the reactionary spirit. Across the South, militant groups like the Ku Klux Klan waged a violent insurgency against the egalitarian governments of the new South. Their violence was paired, even coordinated, with the political activities of the Democratic Party—an inside/outside strategy designed to reinstall the traditional white planter aristocracy at the top of Southern society. Ultimately, the South's reactionary forces outlasted Northern will: in 1877, Republicans agreed to withdraw federal troops from the South in exchange for Democrats conceding defeat in the contested 1876 presidential election.

But the formal end of Reconstruction did not immediately lead to the rise of a new, stable Southern system. In the late 1880s, Blacks and lower-class whites began coalescing in a political alliance against the white elite. The parties representing this cross-racial alliance posed a significant threat to the Democrats in 1894, making it no surprise that the reactionary spirit once again surged across the South. The region's Democratic parties, backed by the old planter elite and new-money industrialists, worked to develop a political order premised on ending Black suffrage and defusing the threat of a cross-racial working-class uprising.

The South's ascendant reactionaries began a series of legal experiments, developing and testing laws that might rig elections in their favor without running afoul of the federal government. Southern Democratic parties codified their successful ideas in a series of constitutional conventions, the first of which was held in Mississippi in 1890. That convention imposed new qualifications on the franchise, such as requiring voters to pay a poll tax and pass a literacy test. These measures,

applied in a nakedly discriminatory fashion, effectively pre-
vented the constituencies supporting the Democrats' rivals
from voting. The now infamous tools became part of the constitutional order across the Southern states, the political controls used to ensure that the new order would not face a serious
electoral threat.

Southern states in the Jim Crow era are sometimes
described as examples of "herrenvolk democracy": a species of
pseudodemocratic system supported by an ethnic or religious
majority group, designed so they and only they can participate.
However, the new Southern systems did not rest on majority
consent among the white population, but rather on a systematic restructuring of elections to ensure that Democrats could
win any election by wide margins *regardless* of public opinion. It was one of history's earliest examples of competitive
authoritarianism.

In his book *Paths out of Dixie*, University of Michigan
political scientist Robert Mickey showed that the South's governments did not depend on majority support from the white
majority. Rather, the regimes maintained themselves on the
basis of a complex web of legal restrictions on ballot access and
civil liberties, paired with brute violence, that disenfranchised
both Blacks and white opponents of the new order. "Suffrage
restriction was a *partisan* project that Democrats strongly
backed but was strongly opposed by the 'vast majority' of
Republicans, third-party politicians, and black activists," he
wrote.

Some of these restrictions, like literacy and poll taxes, are
well known. Others are more obscure. For example, Mickey
noted, some Southern states required that any party nomi-
nate candidates for statewide office through a party primary,
but then only provided public funding for Democratic Party

primaries, making it exceedingly expensive for Republicans or a third party to even field a candidate, let alone contest a general election.

Southern states also imposed strict restrictions on free speech and the press. "Public authorities conducted propaganda campaigns, surveilled the mail and movements of suspected dissidents, and launched legislative investigations and legal attacks on the activities of scores of groups such as the NAACP," Mickey wrote. "Worried about the departure of too many farmworkers [to the North], planters convinced Delta politicians to ban the dissemination of various publications, such as the (black) *Chicago Defender*, which encouraged emigration, as well as the NAACP's *The Crisis*."

Faced with another choice between democracy and protecting hierarchy, the leaders of the American South once again chose hierarchy. But the more democratic national climate required employing means more subtle than reinstating slavery. The South solved this problem by inventing a kind of state-level competitive authoritarianism, an innovation that successfully preserved one-party Democratic rule in the South for decades. Its creation amounted to "the greatest disenfranchisement in the history of democracy," according to political scientist Edward Gibson, who also noted that its "architects" had "no blueprints from other historical cases . . . to draw on."

The American reactionary spirit had adapted itself to new, more thoroughly democratic times. And if you look closely at the historical archive, you can watch this evolution of America's reactionary spirit happen in real time.

The state of Virginia, home to the former capital of the confederacy at Richmond, minuted its convention in a detailed document, the *Report of the Proceedings and Debates of the*

Constitutional Convention of the State of Virginia. Nearly thirty-three hundred pages long, the report contains verbatim transcripts of debates held between June 1901 and June 1902 while the new Jim Crow constitution was being finalized. The one hundred delegates were overwhelmingly Democratic because the party had controlled the nomination process. At the time, Virginia was still governed by a Reconstruction-era constitution. The new convention tasked itself with changing that.

One of the most influential delegates was a Democratic state senator named Carter Glass. A newspaper editor by trade, Glass later became a prominent US senator and secretary of the Treasury under President Woodrow Wilson; he's perhaps best known for writing the Federal Reserve Act and the Glass-Steagall Act, a banking reform law. At the convention, he played a pivotal role in designing the so-called understanding clause, which required citizens to demonstrate a certain level of comprehension of the US Constitution before they would be allowed to vote. The delegates widely understood that this test was to be administered unevenly on the basis of race; according to Glass, that was the point not only of his work but of the entire constitutional convention.

"Discrimination! Why, that is precisely what we propose; that, exactly, is what this Convention was elected for—to discriminate to the very extremity of permissible action under the limitations of the Federal Constitution, with a view to the elimination of every negro voter who can be gotten rid of," he said according to the minutes, boasting that his proposal would "eliminate the darkey as a political factor in this State in less than five years" and ensure "the complete supremacy of the white race in the affairs of government."

In his convention speeches, Glass slipped seamlessly between authoritarian and democratic lines of argument. He was clear-eyed about his objective of mass disenfranchisement, designed both to eliminate Black political power and to ensure that only white men deemed "worthy" could wield that power. Yet Glass was also preoccupied with following legal rules and convinced that he was acting in democracy's best interests. The new constitution, he claimed, would be "the best available expedient to free this Commonwealth from a political system which was devised by its enemies as an instrument of tyranny, and is now utilized by its own citizens for purposes of fraud."

This reference to purported fraud was not a one-off; the Virginia delegates were positively obsessed with the notion that Black suffrage necessarily led to cheating. Alfred P. Thom, a white delegate from the heavily Black city of Norfolk, claimed fraud was so rampant that the current electoral system amounted to "the domination of the Black man" over whites. In Thom's mind, Blacks had been craftily organized to engage in corruption; his speeches are full of alleged statistics on fraudulent votes cast in the state's Black Belt (a collective term for areas with high Black populations). Thom believed that eliminating Black suffrage was a necessary prerequisite for democracy to survive: "The hope that we entertain for fairness of elections is to get rid of the Negro."

The constitution that came out of the convention, which contained the understanding clause and other franchise restrictions like a poll tax, worked largely as Glass and Thom had hoped. The number of eligible Black voters plummeted by about 86 percent after its implementation (from 147,000 to just 21,000). Democrats had a stranglehold on state politics for decades afterward, controlling the governor's mansion until 1970. This was not a surprise; John Summers, a Republican delegate to the convention, warned during the debate that "we leave the Constitutional Convention with an oligarchy."

As Summers recognized, the Virginia constitutional convention was an authoritarian assembly in all but name. It was convened for the purpose of constructing a racial authoritarian state, but it did so in a manner that allowed its delegates to maintain their self-image as good small-*d* democrats. Thom, for example, insisted, "I yield to no one in my purpose to retain a republican form of government in all its sense and all its power in Virginia." He saw no contradiction between this statement and his vociferous advocacy for Black disenfranchisement because, in his telling, the defense of the racial order was essential to defending democracy.

The story of Virginia is the story of the South in miniature. Across the region, white men spoke of freedom and democracy while constructing a system that made a mockery of them. Mickey's research shows, after the wave of new constitutions passed in the South, "candidates for statewide offices could often win election with the support of less than 10 percent of the voting-age population. . . . Until the 1960s, contested general elections in many areas of the South were rare."

America's reactionaries not only had succeeded in protecting racial hierarchy from the various post–Civil War challenges, but had managed to invent a means of doing so that appeared *democratic enough* to weather a more egalitarian national political climate. The architects of the new South knew exactly what they had accomplished and why they had accomplished it. In Alfred Thom's words, "The Anglo-Saxon represents the very aristocracy of the races. It is proud of its position. It is determined to maintain it. And when its domination and supremacy is questioned by any race, and especially by an inferior race, it loses sight of every other question and of every other possibility, and stands with its face to the front until that question is solved and solved forever. That has been its history everywhere."

For decades, it seemed that the "problem" of making post-slavery politics safe for white supremacy may indeed have been "solved forever" by the South's development of competitive authoritarianism. It took a political sea change—decades of civil rights activism and the transformation of the national Democratic Party—for things to truly shift.

OBAMA, TRUMP, AND THE NEW REACTIONARY SPIRIT

Historians of race in America refer to the period between the late 1940s and the 1960s as the Second Reconstruction—and this time, the transformation actually took. The Second Reconstruction shattered the legal, political, and ideological foundations of Southern authoritarianism, a victory with epochal consequences for the whole country. It was, according to the civil rights movement's leaders, a change self-consciously directed at defeating America's authoritarian political tradition.

"Ever since the birth of our nation, white America has . . . been torn between selves—a self in which she proudly professed the great principles of democracy, and a self in which she tragically practiced the antithesis of democracy," Martin Luther King Jr. said in a 1967 speech.

Yet as successful as the civil rights movement proved to be, it did not abolish the reactionary spirit. Instead, it forced the spirit to evolve again—only to reemerge in yet another new form in the twenty-first century.

Legally, the Second Reconstruction created a federal government that was no longer willing to tolerate the existence of competitive authoritarian systems in the states. The 1964 Civil Rights Act and 1965 Voting Rights Act provided the federal government with a bevy of powerful tools—including a functional veto over new voting laws in the South called "preclearance"—that broke local Democratic parties' ability to maintain their lockout of political opponents.

Politically, the Second Reconstruction marked the national Democratic Party's decisive break with its Confederate roots. Beginning with Franklin D. Roosevelt's presidency, the Northern faction of the Democratic Party became increasingly aligned with campaigners for Black rights (owing in part to the growing significance of the Black vote in the North). The Northern faction won out in the Johnson administration, creating the conditions for the passage of the voting and civil rights acts.

Ideologically, the Second Reconstruction changed the way Americans thought about race and social hierarchy. The civil rights movement opened white America's eyes to the evils of racism, making the case that the South's racial caste system simply could not be squared with America's nominal commitments to democracy and human rights. This ideological shift had immediate effects on law and the Democratic Party, but also more far-reaching consequences for America's most basic self-understanding.

In 2001, Harvard sociologist Lawrence Bobo published a paper examining how racial attitudes had shifted in America over the course of the twentieth century. "The single clearest trend," he wrote, was "a steady and sweeping movement toward general endorsement of the principles of racial equality and integration." The percentage of whites who expressed opposition to desegregation and racial intermarriage plummeted after the Second Reconstruction. A hundred years after Alfred Thom declared that "Anglo-Saxons" were willing to do whatever it took to maintain their position of power, the term "white supremacist" had become a slur.

It is hard to overstate how radical this change was. Since the country's founding, and even well before that, belief in racial hierarchy had been a central part of American politics. Yet the Second Reconstruction did for white supremacy what the Civil War did for slavery: rendered it a national enemy, something that no one in the political mainstream could openly promise to bring back. Ex-segregationists who remained in politics, like South Carolina senator Strom Thurmond, had to disavow their old stances in one fashion or another.

"A nation once comfortable as a deliberately segregationist and racially discriminatory society has not only abandoned that view, but now overtly, positively endorses the goals of racial integration and equal treatment. There is no sign whatsoever of retreat from this ideal," Bobo wrote. "The magnitude, steadiness, and breadth of this change should be lost on no one."

But at the same time, Bobo cautioned against concluding that racism had been defeated. The data revealed that white support for racial egalitarianism was thinner than it appeared; on housing, for example, support for living in integrated neighborhoods "decreased as the percentage of Blacks rose." Nearly half of American whites believed stereotypes about Blacks, like the notions that they are "less intelligent" and "hard to get along with." Many whites expressed fear about seeing Blacks on city streets, especially if they were young and male. Whites generally believed that discrimination was not a significant factor in maintaining

Black economic and social disadvantage, despite express-
ing discriminatory attitudes themselves in polling. Instead,
they blamed "the level of effort and cultural patterns of the
minority group members themselves."

Racial hierarchy still had its believers. But they understood
their faith in a different way: less as an affirmative endorsement
of a formal caste system than as a deep hostility to any further
efforts to address persistent inequalities. "The tenacious institutionalized disadvantages and inequalities created by the long
slavery and Jim Crow eras are now popularly accepted and
condoned under a modern free-market or laissez-faire racist
ideology," as Bobo put it.

This was a second major transformation in the reactionary approach to race. Much as Jim Crow emerged to protect
racial hierarchy after the slave-feudal system could no longer
be saved, the new racism emerged to defend what remained of
that hierarchy from further erosion in a world where it could
no longer openly defended.

In this shift, some Republican politicians saw opportunity. The party's leaders correctly believed that voters who
held this kind of attitude were alienated from the newly
pro–civil rights Democrats and could be brought into the
Republican column through a tactic of stoking racial resentment. In a 1981 interview, Republican political strategist Lee
Atwater offered an infamous set of remarks on the scheme's
development:

> You start out in 1954 by saying, "N*gger, n*gger, n*gger." By
> 1968 you can't say "n*gger"—that hurts you, backfires. So
> you say stuff like, uh, forced busing, states' rights, and all
> that stuff, and you're getting so abstract. Now, you're talking
> about cutting taxes, and all these things you're talking

about are totally economic things and a byproduct of them is, blacks get hurt worse than whites. . . . "We want to cut this" is much more abstract than even the busing thing and a hell of a lot more abstract than "N*gger, n*gger."

Atwater's approach worked. By the 2000s, people with racial attitudes that fit Bobo's description of the new racism had overwhelmingly moved into the Republican column— especially, though not exclusively, in the South. A 2016 study by political scientists Avidit Acharya, Matthew Blackwell, and Maya Sen found a direct connection between these voters and previous generations of American reactionaries. "The larger the number of slaves per capita in his or her county of residence in 1860, the greater the probability that a white Southerner today will identify as a Republican, oppose affirmative action, and express attitudes indicating some level of 'racial resentment,'" they wrote. This pattern, the scholars argued, was best explained by racially resentful attitudes being translated between generations all the way back to "the late slave period and the time period after its collapse."

This research provided fairly literal evidence that the reactionary spirit remained at work in America. It showed that support for existing social hierarchies not only can survive massive amounts of egalitarian social change, but also can reassert itself, several generations later, in a politically potent fashion. But the paper didn't explain why and how those attitudes create a threat to democracy today. Reactionary sentiment clearly persisted between the mid-1970s and the 2000s, but no one would have seriously suggested that American democracy was under existential threat from racial reactionaries during that period. So what changed recently?

The answer, in brief, is the election of Barack Obama.

Obama famously did not take an aggressive stance on race during his first presidential run, instead presenting an optimistic story about America overcoming its demons and moving toward a better future. Despite these efforts to assuage white fears surrounding his candidacy, the Obama presidency led to an explosive racist backlash. Michael Tesler, a political scientist at the University of California, Irvine, documented this phenomenon extensively in his book *Post-Racial or Most-Racial?* Tesler's research found that, during the Obama presidency, ordinary citizens' views on nearly everything became shaped by their views on race. It wasn't the way Obama approached the issue while in office that so heavily racialized American politics—in fact, he talked about race less frequently than most presidents did in their first two years—but the mere fact of there being a Black man in office.

In hindsight, it's easy to see why this happened. The presidency is the most important office in the American political system, and by far the most publicly visible. Even people who pay little to no attention to politics tend to know who the president is and have some kind of vague opinion about him. A Black man in the Oval Office is undeniable evidence that *things had changed* in America, that certain elements of the old order no longer held. Obama's victory, paired with mass immigration and declining native-white birth rates, led many older white voters to feel as though they were losing their country—that they had become "strangers in their own land," in sociologist Arlie Hochschild's evocative phrasing.

Race and immigration were not the only factors in creating this sense of alienation. Changing norms around gender and sexuality, a national popular culture heavily focused on the concerns and perspectives of city dwellers, and economic changes like deindustrialization all played at least some role in unsettling America's older rural whites. But there's no doubt that the racial anxieties crystallized by Obama's election were one of the biggest, and most likely *the* biggest, reason for the return of the reactionary spirit in the late 2000s and early 2010s.

This was immediately visible in both the 2009 Tea Party protests and the dominant Republican performance in the 2010 midterm election. In both cases, political scientists have found that racial concerns played a crucial role in motivating the Republican faithful to get involved in politics. The right-wing political turn swiftly yielded antidemocratic legislation in the states. According to the Brennan Center for Justice, twenty-five states imposed new and consequential restrictions on voting between 2010 and 2019, many of which passed swiftly after the 2010 elections, almost exclusively in Republican-controlled statehouses.

Jake Grumbach, a political scientist at the University of California, Berkeley, developed a metric for assessing the health of democracy in all fifty states between 2000 and 2018. Grumbach's index, which covered fifty-one different measures of democracy, found that Republican- and Democratic-run states had relatively similar scores in 2000. But by 2018 the scores had diverged starkly—a phenomenon linked directly to which party was in power. "Results suggest a minimal role for all factors except Republican control of state government, which dramatically reduces states' democratic performance during this period," he wrote. "Republican-controlled governments of states as distinct as Alabama, Wisconsin, Ohio, and North Carolina have [all] taken similar actions with respect to democratic institutions."

Consider North Carolina—a purple state that went for Obama in 2008. Until 2010, it was a relatively high performer on Grumbach's index; after 2010, it took a nosedive and became one of the worst. The principal reason for North Carolina's decline, per his data, was its extreme gerrymander. A federal census was conducted in 2010; as is customary, the next year's state legislature used the results to draw new boundaries for electoral representation in the US House of Representatives and in state-level districts. The maps North Carolina Republicans drew were cartoonishly biased. In the 2010 election, Republicans won a majority of the state's popular vote, leading to seven Republicans and six Democrats representing North Carolina in the US House. In 2012, Democrats won a majority of the state's popular vote in House races—yet Republicans secured a nine-to-four majority in the House delegation. Mathematical analyses show that this Republican bias, which persisted over years, was not plausibly attributable to chance; it had to reflect deliberate choices to rig the game in the GOP's favor. And indeed it did: the private papers of GOP mapmaker Thomas Hofeller, published after his death, contained direct evidence that he had used racial data to draw North Carolina's maps with the intent of weakening the heavily Democratic nonwhite vote.

The North Carolina gerrymandering campaign was supported by a $30 million initiative of the Republican State Leadership Committee called REDMAP (short for Redistricting Majority Project). Launched in 2010, REDMAP supported state Republicans who wished to construct the most aggressive gerrymanders they could. Hofeller himself helped Republicans draw new maps in at least six states other than his own. The US Supreme Court, controlled by Republicans, blessed these practices and other state-level experiments in antidemocracy in 2013, when it gutted the Voting Rights Act's preclearance provision in *Shelby County v. Holder*.

Gerrymandering has been a regrettable feature of American politics for centuries. But almost nothing like this coordinated national effort had been attempted previously. The closest parallel is in the post-Reconstruction South, where redistricting designed to inflate the influence of Democratic-supporting whites was a staple of the Jim Crow competitive authoritarian system.

Moreover, the 2010 gerrymandering wave was paired with a whole slew of new techniques aimed at suppressing the vote. Republican officials around the country purged voters from the registration rolls, enacted stringent new voter ID requirements, and made new rules designed to impede get-out-the-vote efforts. This was not "normal" bare-knuckle politics; something had gone badly wrong in the Republican Party in a very short period of time.

The reactionary spirit had again risen in America and had again adapted itself to a more democratic climate—adopting both a discourse around race and a policy approach that could thrive in the post–civil rights era. The reactionary spirit had grown so strong after Obama that in 2016 its physical embodiment won the race to succeed him.

That Donald Trump's victory was powered in large part by racial anxiety is not seriously in dispute. Some evidence shows that other factors mattered—especially gender and, to a lesser degree, class—but the bulk of the statistical evidence gives race and immigration pride of place in his rise, especially in the Republican primary. A vote for Trump, for many, was a vote against the future, a primal scream directed at a country moving away from the one that his heavily older, heavily white base remembered and toward one they could no longer recognize.

That Trump governed in an antidemocratic fashion is also not seriously in dispute, especially after the 2020 presidential election. Never before had a president refused to accept the legitimacy of his defeat. Never before had a president actively attempted to launch a (quite possibly illegal) scheme to overturn the results of a national election. Never before had a president incited rioters to attack the Capitol in a desperate bid at staying in power.

It's easy for some commentators to blame America's democratic crisis under Trump primarily on the former president's ego and personality flaws. But this is a surface-level analysis. It cannot explain why Republicans engaged in so much antidemocratic behavior before Trump, why the party's voters chose to make Trump their standard-bearer, and why both the party elite and the masses stuck with him through all the obvious misbehavior. These realities are easier to account for if we see Trump more as a *symptom* of a reactionary fever than as its *cause.*

In January 2020, Vanderbilt political scientist Larry Bartels asked more than a thousand Republicans and Republican-leaning independents a series of questions designed to measure support for antidemocratic political ideas. What he found was alarming: a majority agreed that "the traditional American way of life is disappearing so fast that we may have to use force to save it," and a supermajority (73.9 percent) agreed that "it is hard to trust the results of elections when so many people will vote for anyone who offers a handout."

When Bartels dug further into the data, he found that these antidemocratic beliefs were "overwhelmingly" correlated with "ethnocentric concerns about the political and social role of immigrants, African Americans and Latinos in a context of significant demographic and cultural change." Whether a person had concerns about the changing social hierarchy was a better predictor of antidemocratic beliefs than other conservative cultural values or even one's level of support for Trump as president. In supporting Trump, Republicans were making the classic reactionary choice: opting to attack democracy itself rather than accede to democratically authorized social change.

And the GOP remained the party of the reactionary spirit after Biden's inauguration. In 2021, the Brennan Center's data showed nineteen states passing thirty-four different laws infringing on voting rights—the largest number since the organization began keeping tallies. Some of the laws, like Georgia's SB 202, contained especially dangerous provisions, opening the door to partisan interference in the actual counting of votes. The next year, Brennan's data found that another twelve election interference laws went on the books around the country.

In the 2022 midterm elections, the Republican Party nominated roughly 370 candidates for federal or statewide office who rejected or questioned the legitimacy of Biden's 2020 win. These candidates were unusually likely to lose races in competitive states and districts—an important fact we'll examine in some detail in Chapter 7. But at the same time, there are enough noncompetitive races in American politics that the majority of election deniers—nearly 200 candidates— prevailed and are currently in power.

Through all of this, the most egregious antidemocratic behaviors were justified as they always have been in America: as a means of *defending* democracy rather than *attacking* it. In 2020, Trump did not openly claim, Hitler-like, that democracy itself was the problem. Instead, he argued that Biden had stolen the election, and that his supporters needed to act to "stop the steal." Even Georgia governor Brian Kemp, who notably resisted Trump's pressure to undermine the 2020 results in his state, engaged in this kind of fantasy, defending SB 202 on the grounds that "President Biden, the left, and the national media are determined to destroy the sanctity and security of the ballot box."

Modern reactionaries are, by necessity, even more subtle in their defense of hierarchy than their predecessors. No Republican candidate will publicly base their politics on white supremacy in the way that people like John C. Calhoun and Carter Glass did. Racial appeals now are done in code and dog whistles, dressed up in the same sort of conceptual trickery that American authoritarians have long used to mask their antidemocratic aspirations. Sociologist Eduardo Bonilla-Silva once described modern racism as a kind of "racism without racists." Today, the new racial politics has linked up with the long-standing American political tradition of authoritarianism without authoritarians.

This is the second great evolution in America's racial reactionary spirit. The architects of Jim Crow abandoned the formal feudal order but attempted to reinstate it through more subtle legal means; the post-Obama reactionaries reject Jim Crow but use authoritarian means to defend its legacy of a society sharply stratified along racial lines. To say today that slavery and Jim Crow were good, like Scott Terry did at CPAC in 2013, is to render oneself outside the bounds of any respectable politics. But to say, like Milo and Trump have said, that banning Muslim immigration or overturning a legitimate election is actually an expression of America's highest democratic aspirations—that makes you into a Republican Party leader.

As I write this in the winter of 2024, it seems all but inevitable that Donald Trump will once again be the Republican Party's standard-bearer in the coming election. And the threat he poses to American democracy is likely even graver than it was the first time around—not only because of the desperate measures the former president might take to avoid jail time.

When Trump was first elected, he wasn't prepared to actually govern. Beyond a handful of policies like the Muslim ban, he didn't seem to have much in the way of specific ideas for turning his gut-reactionary instincts into policy reality. But by the end of his presidency, Trump had solidified his control over the Republican Party and identified a group of capable staffers who could develop detailed plans for enhancing his personal power over the government. One of the gravest threats was something called Schedule F, an executive order stripping job protections for tens of thousands of civil servants and allowing Trump to replace them with his cronies. The Biden administration stopped Schedule F before it could be implemented, but the Trump camp has developed detailed proposals to bring it back.

In this, Trump and his allies are backed by the might of the institutional conservative movement. Much of the planning for Trump's second term, including detailed legal proposals for enhancing his personal control over government, has been developed by Project 2025, a $22 million initiative led by the Heritage Foundation, a leading conservative think tank. Project 2025's staff has written a handbook nearly one thousand pages long, filled with detailed ideas for transforming the federal government in the event that a Republican takes office in January 2025. It calls not only for reviving Schedule F, but also for demolishing the Justice Department's independence from presidential authority. Given Trump's demonstrated contempt for the idea of nonpolitical government service—as epitomized, for example, by his repeatedly stated desire to use federal law enforcement to go after his political enemies—this amounts to a blueprint for turning the US federal government into a personal tool to enact Donald Trump's whims. Nothing about the Republican primary to this point has hinted at meaningful internal dissent on these issues.

We are witnessing, in real time, the further nationalization of what has been going on at the state and local levels since 2008. The Republican Party, thoroughly controlled by the reactionary spirit, is developing new ways to abuse federal authority and concentrate power in an authoritarian-minded leader's hands—to begin, in short, constructing the scaffolding for a competitive authoritarian system at the federal level. Whether or not a second Trump administration would really succeed in bringing the federal government under his thumb is an open question. But at the very least, its efforts could provide significant cover and support for state-level attacks on democracy—ones that could seriously affect the fairness and competitiveness of national elections for years to come.

There are dozens of reasons why someone might vote Republican in 2024, many of which have nothing to do with race or support for social hierarchy. But at this point, it's clear that the beating heart of the Trump-era GOP—what animates its base and drives its policy agenda into antidemocratic territory—is the American reactionary spirit. The party of Abraham Lincoln has been possessed by the ghosts of Charles II, John C. Calhoun, and Carter Glass. And as a result, democracy itself is on the ballot in 2024.

CHAPTER 3

THE AMERICANIZATION OF THE WORLD

In April 1945, a young man named David Rubin was about to die. A Jewish capmaker from a small town he called Pruzana, today known as Pruzhany in Belarus, Rubin had managed to survive the nightmare of Auschwitz for two years. Fearing the Allied advance, SS soldiers moved Rubin and 1,620 others to Buchenwald, a concentration camp in central Germany, and from there on a death march south into Bavaria. The prisoners were expected to march from five a.m. till around eight p.m. on a diet of two to four potatoes a day; if they attempted to take food from nearby fields, they were shot. They were denied water, drinking what they could find in puddles along the road.

After about two days of torture, they entered a small town outside Munich called Ergoldsbach. A group of regular German army soldiers were in the town, lounging in the street with their vehicles.

Rubin yelled, "Look, look!" to create a distraction, and quickly slid under a tank. He stayed there until the SS guards had gone, about ten minutes later. He then got up and walked toward a local bakery, singing a German song; the Wehrmacht men didn't give him a second glance. For the next two weeks, Rubin lived on scraps scrounged up by a friendly Polish worker; at one point, he hid from German soldiers in a pile of dry dung on a local farm. When the American army liberated the town at the end of the month, a soldier from Chicago found him lying in a street, unable to move his legs. Seeing Rubin's Auschwitz tattoo on his arm, the soldier carried him to a hospital and ordered the Germans to take care of him.

Once he recovered, Rubin became the leader of the small community of Jewish survivors stranded in Ergoldsbach. He recovered the bodies of those who had died nearby and built a Jewish cemetery for them. After presiding over the dedication ceremony, he met an American who worked for the US government's refugee aid branch. The American tracked down a cousin of Rubin's in the United States, a connection that eventually helped Rubin get permission to immigrate. About four years later, he and his new wife, Anita, also a Holocaust survivor, crossed the Atlantic. They settled near David's family in Philadelphia, where their child was born—my mother, Ruth.

Though my grandfather lived with us for several years in my youth, he never talked about any of this with me. I only learned the details of David's extraordinary story in 2011, six years after his death, thanks to a German scholar named Gerhard Strasser. Strasser had been working with residents of Ergoldsbach to document the history of the town during the Holocaust and invited our family to attend a ceremony presenting some of the findings. What I remember from that trip, more than anything else, are the children.

Students at a local school had been assigned projects on Ergoldsbach's Holocaust history, including researching and writing short presentations on Jewish survivors. This wasn't just a normal school assignment; people from around the town came to watch their children recite stories of what had happened. In the audience, I waited anxiously to hear my grandfather's name. Eventually, a German child stood up and told the class about David Rubin's improbable survival and rise to leadership among the survivors.

This was not merely a commemoration; it was repentance. We had been brought to Ergoldsbach, feted and fed, so we could hear members of an entire community confront the darkest chapter of their history—reminding themselves what their people had done and to never do it again. Long after my grandfather ceased to receive official reparation checks from Berlin, the German people were still apologizing to us. An entire society was doing as much as it could to make up for the horrors its ancestors had inflicted on mine. In Ergoldsbach, I felt the weight Germans had put on themselves—and felt moved, as a Jew, that they still cared.

While Americans have long clashed over our country's cruel and bigoted past, Germans have undertaken one of the most thoroughgoing efforts of any nation on the planet to reckon with their history. In her wonderful 2019 book *Learning from the Germans*, Jewish American philosopher Susan Neiman described the development of this *Erinnerungskultur*—"memory culture"—as a "top to bottom" German campaign to transform the country's institutions in the wake of the Nazi catastrophe.

"For several decades, that overhaul has included not only legal examinations and school curricula; it has dominated public debate; created countless works of art, film, literature, and television; and changed the landscape of many German cities," she wrote. "What readmitted Germany to the family of civilized nations only decades after the Holocaust and allowed it to become the leading power in Europe was the recognition of its crimes."

Germany, perhaps more than any other country, has attempted to pull out its homegrown variant of the reactionary spirit by the roots. The Nazis were born out of disgust with post–World War I Weimar democracy, led by men furious about both the new government's weakness and acceptance of the Jewish minority into German society. After Nazism brought Germany to ruin, preventing a reactionary resurgence became one of the central goals of the country's subsequent leaders.

So it's all the more extraordinary that in the past few years, Germany's far right has been on the rise.

In 2015, at the peak of the global refugee crisis, German chancellor Angela Merkel announced an open-door policy for those fleeing violence in Syria and elsewhere. In response, the Alternative for Deutschland (AfD) party, a Euroskeptic faction without a single seat in parliament, morphed into a virulently xenophobic force calling for Germany to slam Merkel's open door shut. In 2017's national elections, AfD won ninety-four seats in the Bundestag, turning it into Germany's third-largest political party.

Opposing the country's approach to the migration policy did not, in and of itself, make AfD a threat to German democracy. But over time the party's behavior has become more and more troubling. In 2020, AfD supporters participated in the attempted storming of the German capitol building, the Bundestag; police charged a former state lawmaker for actions related to the riot. Other rioters came from the Reichsbürger movement, a fringe-right faction that believes every German government since the pre–World War I monarchy has been illegitimate, and that has become increasingly integrated into the AfD itself. In December 2022, German police busted an armed Reichsbürger cell that was plotting to forcibly install a minor noble as Germany's new kaiser. One of the coup plotters was a former AfD member of parliament who was serving in a minor party leadership role at the time of her arrest.

In February 2023, the executive vice president of the International Auschwitz Committee—a Berlin-based antihate group founded by Holocaust survivors—said that "with every year of its existence, the AfD has become increasingly cynical and extreme." Warning of a dire threat to democracy, he compared the party to the Nazis: "They [the AfD] feed and motivate the aggressive attitude of the entire anti-democratic spectrum in Germany. MPs [members of parliament] and representatives of the AfD repeatedly trigger disconcerting memories in the survivors of the German concentration and extermination camps with their speeches and public performances. These memories go far back in time, to when democracy in Germany was openly attacked and mass hatred and anti-Semitism grew on the streets to become an accepted part of everyday life."

Yet AfD's rise has continued. *Politico Europe*'s average of German polls shows that, between July 2022 and 2023, the party's nationwide support nearly doubled—going from 11 percent to 20 percent. By early 2024, AfD was solidly the second-most popular party in Germany; the *Politico* average shows it trailing the center-right Christian Democratic Union (CDU) but leading the ruling Social Democrats by a seven-point margin.

The threat AfD poses to German democracy is, at least to some extent, contained by the German multiparty system. Every mainstream party, most notably including the CDU, has so far refused to consider forming a national governing coalition with the AfD. The far-right faction, while sizable, is not capable of winning control of the German government—at least not yet.

AfD's rise illustrates something vitally important about the reactionary spirit. That Germany, of all countries, could fail to prevent a surge in reactionary antidemocratic politics suggests there's something eternal and enduring about the reactionary spirit—and something about our current time period that makes it especially likely to flourish.

To fully account for the rise of AfD and parties like it around the world, we need to answer two crucial questions. First, what is it about the world today that has made it possible for so many antidemocratic factions to gain power in seemingly stable democracies? Second, why do these factions all present themselves less like fascists and more like traditional American authoritarians, wrapping themselves in democracy's banner? Both can be answered by looking at the same basic development: democracy's emergence as the only viable political ideology over the last century.

Democracy's global rise during the late twentieth and early twenty-first centuries came alongside the global spread of associated ideas, like political equality and human rights. These ideas helped fuel a sweeping set of challenges to existing social hierarchies in countries across the world, ranging from decolonization to the feminist and LGBT movements to campaigns for religious tolerance. Such sweeping transformations were bound to trigger a powerful surge in the reactionary spirit, and indeed they did.

In order to succeed in a world now dominated by democracy and its core principle of equality, modern reactionaries generally could not directly attack democracy the way that fascists once did. So reactionaries began donning the kind of democratic guise long worn by their American peers. While the United States was once exceptional in its national commitment to democracy, it has recently become representative. And as the world became more ideologically American, so, too, did its authoritarians.

THE NAZI LAWYER WHO SAW THE FUTURE

In the late eighteenth and early nineteenth centuries, democracy was a revolutionary cause. The American and French Revolutions revealed that Europe's established monarchies faced a new threat from below—one that threatened not only to change the political system, but also to enact a wholesale transformation in the distribution of wealth, power, and social status. European reactionaries rose up swiftly to contain it; the years 1815 to 1848 are often termed "the age of reaction," defined by a concerted transnational effort by European elites to repress the rising liberal-democratic tide.

The reactionary spirit in early-modern Europe was very different from its equivalent across the Atlantic. While John C. Calhoun was proclaiming his commitment to the revolutionary ideals of freedom and democracy, Calhoun's European peers—like Austrian foreign minister Klemens von Metternich, architect of the post-1815 European political order—openly described democracy as the enemy they aimed to defeat. Democracy is "a reality—*une vérité*—in America. In Europe it is a falsehood, and I hate all falsehood," Metternich told an American journalist in 1836.

The age of Metternichian reaction concluded with the revolutions of 1848, a wave of democratic uprisings that upended politics on the continent. Though these revolutions mostly failed to durably replace monarchies with democracies, they proved that the central monarchical principle—the notion that political power flowed from divine and natural grants of power to a chosen elite—was losing its grip on the hearts and minds of the European public. After 1848, European reactionaries increasingly felt the need to contest elections and employ American-style democratic rhetoric to win them—gradual signs of a collapse in ancien régime legitimacy that became undeniable after World War I.

That war was not really about democracy. It was triggered by European geopolitics and arcane alliance agreements more than anything else. But the leaders of the Western Allied powers—especially US president Woodrow Wilson—were happy to use democracy as an ideological justification for their war effort. Wilson, who famously declared that an Allied victory would "make the world safe for democracy," worked to ensure that the postwar order would be a democratic one—and for a moment, it seemed that he may have been successful. The leading Central Powers opponents—Wilhelmine Germany and the Austro-Hungarian Empire—were wracked by democratic and nationalist revolution. By 1920, democracies dominated the ranks of Europe's leading European powers. The age of monarchical rule was over for good.

"The history of political and state theory in the nineteenth century could be summarized with a single phrase: the triumphal march of democracy," a young German legal theorist named Carl Schmitt wrote in 1923. "No state in the Western European cultural world withstood the extension of democratic ideas and institutions."

Schmitt wasn't celebrating these developments; his 1923 book, titled *The Crisis of Parliamentary Democracy*, advanced a lacerating, prescient critique of contemporary democracy.

For Schmitt, democracy's triumph over monarchy would not produce political stability. In fact, he argued, its victory was already giving rise to a new kind of ideological struggle—between democracy and liberalism.

During the fight against monarchy, democracy and liberalism were fully aligned: to believe in popular sovereignty was to believe in replacing absolute monarchy with a system that held elections and protected liberal freedoms. But in Schmitt's mind, this connection was more historical happenstance than conceptual necessity. Democracy, he believed, could not be seen as requiring rights and even universal suffrage in the way liberals understood them.

A government is democratic, he argued, if it bases its legitimacy on the popular will. But what that means depends on how you define the people and how you assess their will. Every democracy has excluded some people from voting, most notably foreigners; that means, by definition, no democracy has ever rested on universal human equality before the law. Instead, the idea of equality in democracy really means equality among a specific political community—one defined by the fact that its members share a certain core identity.

"Every actual democracy rests on the principle that not only are equals equal but unequals will not be treated equally. Democracy requires, therefore, first homogeneity and second—if the need arises—elimination or eradication of heterogeneity," Schmitt wrote in a 1926 preface to the second edition of *Crisis*. "There has never been a democracy that did not recognize the concept 'foreign' and that could have realized the equality of all men." Universal equality, Schmitt insisted, is a liberal concept rather than a democratic one, and "modern mass democracy rests on the confused combination of both."

Schmitt argued that we must reject liberal universality and instead recognize that politics is *always* about defining who is a "friend" (inside the political community) and who is an "enemy" (outside of it, and therefore a potential target in war). This is as true in democracy as in any other form of government, thus bringing it into necessary conflict with liberalism—a doctrine that seeks to supplant conflict and exclusion, the true essences of politics, with impossible attempts at universal inclusion.

The tension between liberal idealism and democratic reality is the source of the "crisis" in his book's title. Democracy's ideological triumph after World War I forced a reckoning with the ways in which actual politics clashed with stated liberal principles. "Democracy and liberalism could be allied to each other for a time . . . but as soon as it achieves power, liberal democracy must decide between its elements," Schmitt wrote. "The crisis of the modern state arises from the fact that no state can realize a mass democracy, a democracy of mankind."

Schmitt had (unintentionally) elevated the principles of America's slave drivers and segregationists into a universal credo. He wrote a blueprint, adaptable virtually anywhere, for how to engage in reactionary politics while claiming to be fighting on democracy's behalf.

Where Calhoun argued that American democracy depended on keeping Blacks in chains, Schmitt claimed that *every* democracy depended on excluding *someone* in some manner. It did not matter, for Schmitt, what the reasons for that exclusion were. "Every religious, moral, economic, ethical, or other antithesis transforms into a political one if it is sufficiently strong to group human beings effectively according to friend and enemy," he wrote in his 1932 book *The Concept of the Political*.

What does matter is that the state *decide* on one of these distinctions—religious, ethnic, whatever—and then insist on it as the dividing line between friend and enemy. The political community is created through this act of decision, the distinction between inside and outside. So long as the people inside support the government, it can claim the mantle of democracy. The opinions of those outside its homogeneous political community do not matter, even if they live inside the state's borders. Potentially, they may even be the domestic "enemy"— groups whose members can be legitimately marginalized, warred upon, and even exterminated.

Here you can see the terrible genius of Schmitt's argument. He has provided a scheme for something called "democratic politics" that replaces universal equality, the foundational idea of democracy as we understand it, with hierarchy—specifically, the placement of one group over all others. Democratic equality, for Schmitt, is "the equality of equals" and "the will of those who belong to the equals." Those outside the group suffer what they must.

By positioning his argument not as a monarchist attack on democracy but as a democratic attack on liberalism, he invented an authoritarian politics perfectly suited to an era when democratic ideals dominated. And make no mistake: Schmitt's own preferred politics were indeed authoritarian, whatever language he used to describe them. In *Crisis*, he argued that there is nothing about democracy that requires elections or even parliaments; dictatorships, in his mind, can be perfectly democratic provided they can find some way to show they have popular approval among a homogeneous community. "The will of the people can be expressed just as well and perhaps better through acclamation, through something taken for granted, an obvious and unchallenged presence, than through the statistical apparatus that has been constructed with such meticulousness in the last fifty years," he wrote.

For this reason, he claimed that communism and fascism were "certainly antiliberal but not necessarily antidemocratic." Even though Schmitt admitted that "Italian Fascism seems to place no value on being 'democratic'" in its rhetoric, he still thought its attempts to appeal to a homogeneous group of Italians and build a mass political state fell under the democratic umbrella.

Less than a decade after the publication of *Crisis*, Schmitt applied similar logic to celebrate the new Nazi state. While initially skeptical of National Socialism, to the point where he argued in 1932 that the Weimar state would be justified in using force to crush Hitler's movement, he soon joined the party and worked (with the patronage of Hermann Göring) to develop the Third Reich's legal code. It certainly helped that Schmitt was a lifelong anti-Semite; after the Nuremberg Laws stripping Jews of citizenship rights were enacted in 1935, Schmitt praised the Nazi regime for freeing German law from the domination of "parasites," saying, "Today the German people has . . . become the German people again." (Notably, the Nuremberg Laws were partly patterned on Jim Crow.)

At this point, Schmitt had clearly abandoned any commitment he once had to even the pretense of supporting democracy. But despite his newfound enthusiasm for Nazism, the Nazis had less enthusiasm for him. In December 1936, the official newspaper of the SS denounced Schmitt as (among other

things) a Hegelian and false anti-Semite. While never perse-
cuted exactly, he did not play an important role in the Nazi
regime in the critical years to come.

The Nazis didn't really need Schmitt. His thinking was better suited for a more ambiguous time, one where authoritarian
politics needed to operate with more subtlety and intellectual
finesse than the rank bigotry of Hitler and the murderous
brawn of the SS. Schmitt's chief insight into democracy was
seeing how the politics of illiberal groupism, of replacing "all
men are created equal" with "friend and enemy," could justify a brand of authoritarian politics in seemingly democratic
terms. He identified a truly difficult intellectual challenge for
liberal democracy—how can you square the credo of universal human rights with the inherently limited nature of national
citizenship and borders?—and pushed on it to develop an
argument for a seductive brand of authoritarian politics.

The years after World War II called for a return to reactionary subtlety. The Nazi defeat, and the subsequent revelation of
what they had done to Jews like my grandparents, thoroughly
discredited the European far right. A handful of postwar political parties tried to keep the fascist flame alive, but nearly all
of them failed to achieve any electoral success whatsoever. The
two remaining fascist-aligned dictatorships on the continent,
Spain and Portugal, distanced themselves from the discredited
ideology.

Yet the reactionary spirit did not die with Hitler and Mussolini. The postwar order's push for greater social equality
would generate resistance from those who preferred that things
stay the way they were. The political style that emerged would
bear an eerie resemblance to Carl Schmitt's: a reactionary politics centered on what he termed "the inescapable contradiction
of liberal individualism and democratic homogeneity."

HOW THE LATE TWENTIETH CENTURY SET THE STAGE
FOR REACTIONARY REBIRTH

Political scientists often separate the rise of democracy into three broad waves. The first dates from the early nineteenth century to the years immediately following World War I. The second begins immediately after World War II, defined by the rebirth of democracy in western Europe and its emergence in a handful of postcolonial states. This would soon be eclipsed by a massive third wave beginning in the 1970s and lasting for somewhere around forty years. During this period, dictatorships of both the right and the left fell almost everywhere: Latin America, East Asia, sub-Saharan Africa, and the Eurasian countries of the former Eastern Bloc. By the turn of the century, roughly half of all countries around the world were democracies.

Democracy seems so normal, from a contemporary perspective, that it's easy to lose sight of just how stunning this transformation was. In the long arc of human history, democracy is a recent newcomer; some variant of authoritarianism has been the default setting of human government for thousands of years. But in a little more than half a century, democracy went from nearly extinct—just twelve democracies survived the Second World War—to globally dominant. No single political system had ever conquered the entire planet so rapidly or so thoroughly.

Looking from that historical vantage point, it would be surprising if democracy's rise did not produce authoritarian challenges. Indeed, each wave of democracy had its share of failures, a swift return to authoritarianism in many countries that had recently been democratized. These failed transitions took place in countries where democracy was new and not yet institutionalized, weaker systems easily overthrown by outright authoritarian enemies like military juntas.

But in countries where democracy had a long history, or seemed to establish itself quickly and thoroughly, democratic reversals were quite rare. In fact, they were unheard of prior to the twenty-first century. To understand how the reactionary spirit grew so strong in seemingly robust democracies, like the United States and India, we need to take a closer look at what happened during its postwar rise. During this period, events refuted Schmitt's prediction of a divorce between democracy and liberalism. Not only did liberal forms of democracy spread globally, but the number of groups included in democratic polities expanded. Women became bigger players in society and public life. New welfare states distributed the benefits of rapid economic growth to the poor like never before. The LGBT community asserted its right to exist and be treated with dignity and respect.

Among these many important moves toward social equality, two stand out as especially consequential for the reemergence of the reactionary spirit: the dissolution of European empires, and (somewhat related) mass migrations of people around the globe.

The archetypal European empire was a democracy for its citizens at home uneasily paired with authoritarian systems in the colonies. Western Europe's claims to be defending democracy during the world wars were always marred by the nations' insistence on governing a population of millions, sometimes larger than their own, under brutal imperial regimes. Schmitt himself saw the British Empire as striking evidence that politics depended on exclusion in even the most established democracies. When these regimes ended, the opportunity was there for dozens of new countries to emerge as democratic states—and for the reactionary spirit to emerge as an obstacle in their path.

Few colonial states became democracies immediately after independence and stayed that way. Building a democratic political system is difficult, requiring people who have deep and profound differences to treat each other as partners in governing rather than as Schmittian enemies. Many postcolonial regimes were set up for failure: colonial powers often intentionally elevated one social group over others as part of a divide-and-conquer strategy. After independence, such tensions between social groups—whether rooted in race, class, ethnicity, religion, or some combination of the above—frequently contributed to the failure of the new democracies.

Israel and India were notable exceptions to this general pattern. Both founded in the late 1940s, and both declaring allegiance to democracy in their founding documents, they are the two oldest democracies outside the Western world. Theoretically, they should be two of the most well-established democracies in the world. Yet both were, from the outset, riven by conflict over hierarchy and identity. Israel struggled with how to cohere its identity as a Jewish democracy with divisions inside the Jewish community and, more fundamentally, with the Arab Palestinian minority. India was founded as a secular state of all its citizens but still faced similar challenges, particularly with respect to caste divisions and its large Muslim population. Thus, both of these postcolonial "success stories" were set up for surges in the reactionary spirit—ones potentially powerful enough to threaten the foundations of their seemingly well-established democracies.

Imperial collapse did not just transform life in the former colonies; it also fundamentally challenged former colonial powers' sense of place in the family of nations. European nations were increasingly forced to meet all the other countries as equals on the world stage, the first time they'd needed to do so in centuries. More than that, actually: they had to welcome former subjects into their homelands. In the decades after the Second World War, many European nations faced a labor shortage that required new workers to keep the economy growing. Many of these workers came from the former colonies, places where the people spoke the language of their colonizers.

Decolonization and migration were powerful forms of egalitarian social change. They not only challenged the greatest source of global inequality, the gap between residents of rich and poor countries, but also existentially unsettled the way white European majorities understood social hierarchy, both globally and domestically. For some it was a shattering event—one that created a political opening for the reactionary spirit's resurgence.

The first politician to truly seize on this opportunity was a Frenchman named Jean-Marie Le Pen. In the 1950s, Le Pen was a politician as well as a soldier in the French Foreign Legion. He served in France's bloody colonial wars in Vietnam and Algeria. For the next several decades, he labored to build an extreme-right party back home in France. In 1972, he founded the Front National (FN), a party that came to focus almost monomaniacally on the threat from immigration. By attacking immigrants and their children under the FN slogan "France is for the French," Le Pen could galvanize appeal to the same sense of status and social threat that had previously buoyed fascists without owning the toxic label. Le Pen and his allies argued that African migrants from France's former colonies, especially Muslim migrants, could not be assimilated into French culture; they would be unproductive citizens who brought crime and threatened the Schmittian homogeneity of the French nation. Much like his American contemporary Lee Atwater, Le Pen had developed a way of recycling old racialized fears in a package better suited to a more egalitarian cultural context.

These anti-immigrant arguments were intimately bound up with the postcolonial sense of loss experienced by many French citizens, a belief that their nation had lost an essential part of what had made it great. The extremely violent war to retain its Algerian colony had ended in 1962, only a decade before the FN's founding, so the wound to the French national psyche was fresh. The FN worked hard to link immigration to decolonization, arguing that mass migration from former colonies constituted a form of *colonisation à rebours* (reverse colonization) forced on the country by left-wing elites. By permitting this migration, he argued, elites were acting out of a misplaced sense of white guilt, blinded to the essential justness of French colonization by corrosive left-wing ideology.

These arguments proved powerful. In the 1984 European Parliament elections, held roughly a dozen years after the FN's founding, the party won 11 percent of the French vote. In 2002, Le Pen placed second in France's presidential election, taking incumbent Jacques Chirac to a runoff. His daughter Marine, who took over leadership of the party after his retirement, has now repeated that feat—cementing the status of the party, whose name she later changed to National Rally, as the major rival to current president Emmanuel Macron. After the 2022 legislative elections, National Rally became the third-largest party in France's legislature; polling suggests she might well be the frontrunner in the 2027 presidential contest.

The French far right's successes proved to be the beginning of a revolution. In the 1970s and 1980s, Europe's extreme right seemed like a spent force in mass politics. Le Pen's development of a way forward—xenophobia with an appeal to national greatness and whitewashed history—rapidly diffused across the continent. Far-right parties like Austria's FPÖ (Freedom Party) found electoral success by adopting key elements of the FN's messages on immigration and history.

Data from Matt Golder, a political scientist at Penn State University, illustrates just how successful this project was. Between 1985 and 1990, he found, the national vote share of FN-style far-right parties roughly quadrupled while the vote share of neofascist parties stayed flat. The data reveals the importance of the far right avowing respect for democracy and repudiating naked racism, positions that convinced millions of Europeans they were something other than neofascists. Scholars have identified this "reputational shield"—a European far-right party's ability to plausibly distance itself from overt fascism—as essential to its success.

The rapid growth of reactionary factions in Europe in the 1980s showed that the FN's success was not the result of a unique French political culture. Decolonization and mass migration had created a continent-wide cultural shock, a one-two-punch threat that fed off both discomfort with changing societies and an existential fear that Europe had lost its place.

A paper by two economists, Beatrice Brunner and Andreas Kuhn, identified the political power of European culture shock by examining forty years of data on Swiss elections. It turned out that support for anti-immigrant policies and parties didn't track immigration exactly; immigration by people from nearby European countries who spoke languages used in Switzerland didn't really matter. Instead, it was immigration by "culturally different" migrants—most notably, non-Europeans—that seemed to have been behind the rising support for anti-immigrant politics during the period they studied.

"Part of the native population appears to perceive culturally different immigrants as threatening their national identity, i.e. their culture, their language, religion, and their way of life in general," Brunner and Kuhn concluded. "[In this], Switzerland is by no means a special case with respect to attitudes toward immigration when compared with other European countries."

Of course, the reactionary spirit is more specific than mere right-wing politics. It is the curdling of support for traditional social structures and hierarchies into opposition to democracy itself. The mere fact that far-right parties in Europe succeeded by demonizing immigrants did not, in and of itself, prove that the reactionary spirit was rising again in Europe.

But as we saw in the United States, these parties' pledges of support for democracy did not guarantee that they truly supported democratic values. When openly challenging democracy is a political death sentence, virtually everyone who hopes to one day wield power will claim its mantle. The FN's example proved that the new far right could indeed succeed by following a Schmittian blueprint: describing non-European immigrants as the internal "enemy" and thus turning nascent fears about social change among a segment of the European population into a potent political force. Because this kind of politics attacked democracy's core political value of equality, it created space for outright antidemocratic factions (a label appropriate for some, albeit not all, of the new European far right) to credibly compete for power.

Far-right politics in Europe had thus become American-
ized: fully adapted to conditions where democracy was the
only game in town, and ideologically equipped to serve as a
political vehicle for the reactionary spirit. But this brand of
reactionary politics had not yet attracted a large enough support base to become truly dangerous, either in the Atlantic
world or in other consolidated democracies. That would happen in the next few decades—an era that would turn the reactionary spirit into an existential threat to democracy around
the world.

REACTION AT HISTORY'S END

After the Berlin Wall fell in 1989, it appeared that the
twentieth-century triumph of democracy was complete. Having defeated fascism, its rival on the right, and communism, its
rival on the left, Western-style liberal democracy truly faced
no challenger. Its spread around the globe seemed assured.

And for a few years, it was. The 1990s saw some of the
most significant activity of democracy's third wave, including across nearly all of Eastern Europe. Former communist states and Soviet republics—like Czechia, Hungary, and
Estonia—democratized with remarkable speed. In some countries, the new democratic systems appeared to be fully stable in
less than a decade.

In ideological terms, the world appeared mostly Ameri-
canized in the sense that democracy was the barely contested
benchmark by which governments were measured. This was
not true literally everywhere: culturally and locally specific
antidemocratic ideologies remained influential in countries
like China and Iran. But governments like the ones in those

nations did not present any kind of plausible or attractive alternative vision for most people around the world. On the whole, the language of democracy—human rights, elections, free speech, individual autonomy—became the assumed argot of global politics.

This time period is often described as the "end of history," largely thanks to a 1989 essay and subsequent book by political theorist Francis Fukuyama. Fukuyama argued that liberal democracy was the ultimate stage in the evolution of society. Fundamental forces in history, including deep human desires for recognition and equality, had buoyed it to global dominance.

Contrary to some common caricatures, Fukuyama did not claim that this state of affairs would necessarily last forever. Instead, he predicted, the very triumph of the system contained the seeds of a future crisis. "No regime—no 'socioeconomic system'—is able to satisfy all men in all places. This includes liberal democracy," he wrote in the book. "Dissatisfaction arises precisely where democracy has triumphed most completely: it is a dissatisfaction *with* liberty and equality. Thus those who remain dissatisfied will always have the potential to restart history."

Some of this "dissatisfaction" was visible soon after the Cold War's end. In the 1990s, the far right began making its presence felt in a handful of European elections: Austria's Freedom Party even entered a governing coalition in 2000 after a strong showing in the 1999 election. The 2000s and early 2010s saw varying signs of antidemocratic activity in consolidated democracies, from both the religious right (Recep Tayyip Erdogan's consolidation of power in Turkey) and the socialist left (Hugo Chavez's attack on democracy in Venezuela).

But as the 2010s wore on, it became clear that something new was happening on the right across advanced democracies. The far right had risen to power in the United States, Hungary, Israel, India, Brazil, and Poland. Extreme-right western European parties—some of which, like Germany's AfD, had a tenuous relationship at best with democracy—enjoyed an unprecedented wave of electoral success, winning larger seat shares in parliaments and joining governing coalitions in larger numbers.

Every one of these new authoritarian movements presented itself as deeply and authentically democratic. While the parties openly attacked democracy-adjacent values—like liberalism, multiculturalism, or secularism—they all insisted that they supported the basic ideas of popular sovereignty and elections. This strategy reflected the enduring global democratic consensus: a 2017 Pew survey of people in thirty-eight countries found that huge majorities, a country median of 78 percent, believed that "a democratic system where representatives elected by citizens decide what becomes law" was a good way to run a country. Recognizing this reality, autocrats around the world began singing a more democratic tune.

In their 2022 book *Spin Dictators*, political scientists Sergei Guriev and Daniel Treisman quantitatively documented a transformation in global authoritarianism: a movement away from overt violent repression and toward manufacturing consent through ersatz elections and a managed press. Guriev and Treisman noted that this trend had even touched countries like Russia and Singapore, where public support for democracy as a governing system is far weaker than it is in the United States or western Europe. This, they argued, has a lot to do with democracy's post-twentieth-century ideological dominance: in an interconnected planet where large portions of the world's governments and citizens take democratic ideals seriously, even the most hardened authoritarian can face tangible consequences for open crackdowns on rights and freedoms.

The result was that political movements everywhere, but especially ones in seemingly consolidated democracies, had powerful incentives to develop a democratic-sounding justification for their actions—to Americanize their politics in the way that Schmitt theorized and the FN pioneered. By identifying domestic "enemies" that stood in for unwanted social change, they learned to galvanize a chunk of the public against those enemies in the name of protecting the homogeneous majority—an ironically universal playbook for antidemocratic success.

But while studying the rhetoric of these new authoritarian movements helps explain *how* they appealed to a mass audience, it doesn't explain *why* people were especially attracted to their political vision *today*. The theory of the reactionary spirit helps us understand this phenomenon. It also clarifies why far-right parties of a certain sort, and not, say, neo-Nazis or the Trotskyite left, were best positioned to succeed in our current political climate.

Throughout the postwar era, but especially in the past thirty years, the deep logic of democracy has fueled powerful challenges to the unequal distributions of wealth, power, and social standing. As democracy's reach expanded across the globe, so, too, did political contests over inequality. That competition, one way or another, brought tensions over status and identity to the fore of the political conversation—ideal circumstances for the reactionary spirit to threaten democracies old and new.

This is the underlying structural reality that helped the authoritarian right break through in country after country. Under such conditions, all it would take to start a reactionary fire was some kind of spark: an external shock, a high-visibility left-wing push for social change, canny leadership on the reactionary side, or some combination of all three (as in the United States in the post-Obama era). The 2010s saw a series of such trigger events around the world: decades of democratic expansion and evolving reactionary responses leading to a simultaneous surge in support for reactionary factions.

In Hungary and elsewhere in Europe, the 2015 refugee crisis played a central role in the story. That year, violent bloodshed in countries like Syria and Afghanistan produced the single greatest number of refugees since World War II, many of whom fled to Europe seeking a better life. The centrist European establishment, led by German chancellor Angela Merkel, chose to welcome them, creating an opportunity for far-right parties to increase their support among Europeans uncomfortable with a massive influx of people who looked different, prayed differently, and spoke different languages. The effect was swift and striking: data from The PopuList, which catalogs far-right electoral support in European elections since 1989, shows a spike in these factions' support around the continent in the wake of the crisis.

Broadly speaking, the evidence suggests that European resentment toward immigration is rooted in concerns about changes to Europe's traditional ethnic composition and hierarchy. A 2007 study that examined twenty European countries and over thirty-eight thousand individuals found that negative attitudes about multiculturalism were by far the best predictor of individual opposition to immigration. Many other factors, like a country's unemployment level or a person's individual income, had a negligible effect.

This underlying hostility toward cultural difference created fertile grounds for far-right parties to profit from a sudden spike in immigrant numbers, especially since many immigrants came from nonwhite Muslim countries. A 2018 paper by two German political scientists, Matthias Mader and Harald Schoen, examined a survey that asked the same group of people their opinions on elections and immigration before and after the refugee crisis. They found that attitudes on immigration, on the whole, hadn't changed much: the same people who disliked immigration before the crisis still did afterward. But their partisan allegiances had shifted dramatically; anti-immigrant voters who had supported Merkel's CDU defected to the AfD in significant numbers.

This is the reactionary spirit in action. The refugee crisis heightened the stakes for culturally conservative voters, forcing them to choose between centrist parties that were more welcoming to migrants and potentially antidemocratic extremists who opposed it. Many of them chose the latter, prioritizing preserving the traditional white-dominant society over protecting their democracy. Across Europe, the parties that had been following Le Pen's blueprint started to reap electoral dividends. In Hungary in particular, the surge in power of anti-immigrant politics allowed a government that had already moved in an authoritarian direction to push a new and potent propaganda line, harnessing the reactionary spirit to consolidate its hold on power.

Similar events took place outside Europe. Post–Cold War Israel went through multidecade struggles over its ethnoreligious identity and occupation of Palestinian land, ultimately creating conditions for the reactionary spirit to spread from a small handful of extremists to a significant portion of the population. In India, the reactionary right's rise began with a staged crisis designed to bring out the Hindu majority's unease with India's vision of equality.

Fukuyama's warning has proved prescient. Frustration with the dominant era of equality and liberal rights kept history going, with the reactionary spirit threatening democracy in its strongholds at a moment when democracy's grip on the world looked solid.

In the coming chapters, we'll examine in much greater detail how this new reactionary politics works: the precise techniques reactionaries use to subtly weaken democracy, the kinds of social divisions that enable reactionary triumph, and what the reactionary spirit's global rise means for democracy's long-term future worldwide. But before we move on, we need to talk about an alternative theory of our current democratic crisis, one focusing not on identity but on economics.

(DON'T) FOLLOW THE MONEY

Around the same time that democracy conquered the globe, a new economic ideology became dominant in the advanced democratic world. Neoliberalism, as it's now called, championed free markets, free trade, deregulation, and the privatization of government services. Neoliberalism profoundly reshaped the global economy in the latter decades of the twentieth century, leading to the elimination of trade barriers and the weakening of welfare states across the democratic world.

This new economic order had its advantages. Some developing countries, most notably India and China, benefited immensely from access to global markets—and their growth contributed to an unprecedented decline in poverty worldwide. But at the same time, the developed world became more unequal. In Europe and particularly the United States, the lower middle class suffered from the weakened social safety net and the departure of factory jobs to poorer countries with cheaper labor costs. Entire communities were impoverished; drug and alcohol abuse rose.

It makes sense that some see this as the root cause of the modern rise of reactionary politics; in the long arc of history, there are plenty of examples of extreme economic inequality destabilizing nations. On this theory, the rage and resentment of working-class people toward the elites who benefited under neoliberalism built and built and built while politicians did little to address their grievances. Rising hostility to diversity and immigration, on this account, is not an ideological backlash against equality per se but rather a displaced fury at decades of economic dispossession.

This "economics-first" account is totally plausible in the abstract, and it's easy to see why so many political commentators have gravitated toward it. Putting economics first humanizes the supporters of extreme and even antidemocratic parties, helping mainstream observers comprehend voting choices that strike them as otherwise indefensible or even immoral. For this reason, versions of the economics-first narrative immediately emerged as one of the dominant explanations for the twin 2016 shocks of Trump and Brexit.

However, this theory only makes sense in a Western context. It has a hard time explaining why some countries that have seen rapid economic growth, like India and Israel, have also seen surges in antidemocratic politics. In these countries, it's greater *prosperity* that seems to have laid the groundwork for a surge in reactionary politics, not rising impoverishment or even inequality. And indeed, detailed research from experts on these countries confirms that the reactionary right's base is not coming from a place of economic deprivation.

Nissim Mizrachi, a sociologist at Tel Aviv University, studied voters from the marginalized Mizrahi Jewish community, who form the base of Prime Minister Benjamin Netanyahu's Likud party. He found that their support was primarily rooted not in their economic deprivation, but in a sense that the Israeli left's idea of universal equality threatens core elements of Israel's distinctively Jewish character.

"The right-wing bloc attaches far greater importance to Jewish identity than to democratic identity. This is a local identity that is bound up with the Jewish people—with everything related to the defense of the state's Jewish identity before everything else," Mizrachi said in a 2020 interview with the newspaper *Haaretz*. "It's a categorical error to think that Likud voters are just sitting around waiting for some sort of dialogue of redemption that will forge equality between poor and rich."

A paper by Pavithra Suryanarayan, a political scientist at the London School of Economics, examined support in India for the Hindu nationalist BJP faction among the Brahmin (or Brahman) caste, which sits at the top of the country's caste hierarchy. She found that concern for preserving caste privilege was a major driver of BJP support, even among poor Brahmins who would benefit from the Indian National Congress party's relatively more redistributionist policies.

Research suggests that similar dynamics are at work in the West. In their 2019 book *Cultural Backlash*, political scientists Pippa Norris and Ronald Inglehart examined decades of data on political attitudes among American and European voters—all with an eye toward explaining why what they call "authoritarian populist" parties have been on the rise. They found that economics has steadily receded in political salience inside Western democracy. The most important issues and key divisions between parties increasingly center on race, gender, migration, and the environment.

Norris and Inglehart argued that the rise of "postmaterial" politics, as they term it, is at root a product of rising prosperity. After World War II, economies boomed across the Western world, leading to an unprecedented increase in living standards. While the benefits of this growth became more unequally divided in the neoliberal era, the average American or western European was still substantially wealthier than they had been in 1945. According to Norris and Inglehart, people who grew up in the new era of abundance were less inclined to prioritize economic issues in voting; their most basic material needs were being met, and their formative experiences acculturated them into caring about socially liberal causes. As these younger voters came of age, they began agitating for liberal cultural change, breeding backlash from older, more conservative generations. In this way, it was economic growth rather than rising inequality that set the stage for the reactionary spirit's return.

Cultural Backlash presents an impressive amount of data to support this argument, including a massive dataset on European political attitudes and voting behavior (covering roughly 332,000 individuals in thirty-two countries between 2002 and 2014). The authors' regression analyses found that culture, not class, was the key distinction between those who supported reactionary parties and those who did not. "Several economic indicators, such as occupational class and subjective financial insecurity, turn out to be statistically significant but relatively weak predictors," they wrote. "Overall, cultural values . . . are more closely related to voting support than economic indicators."

Norris and Inglehart are not scholarly outliers. While pundits have been more drawn to an economics-first story, the bulk of the academic research in both Europe and the United States supports more of a culture-first story, one where economic inequality may play a role in the rise of far-right authoritarian politics, but a relatively marginal role compared with the core conflicts over hierarchy and identity.

Much of the key research in this area focuses on Donald Trump's victories in the Republican primary and the 2016 general election. This body of work cannot explain every component of the Trump phenomenon, such as the rise in nonwhite support for his candidacy in 2020, but it is not designed to. Rather, it helps us make sense of the foundations of Trump's enduring electoral strength: the committed supporters who helped him take over the Republican Party in 2016, outmuscle Hillary Clinton in the general election, and then hold the GOP in thrall for all the years to come. When it comes to Trump's base, the priority of identity over economics is economically clear.

One good example from this vast literature is a 2018 paper by Brian Schaffner, Matthew MacWilliams, and Tatishe Nteta focusing on white voters without college degrees, the decisive bloc in flipping the election in Trump's direction. They used a battery of questions to assess different voters' views of race, gender, and their own personal economic situation, and then sifted through the data to connect these traits to Trump and Clinton voters. The evidence was clear. "While economic considerations were an important part of the story, racial attitudes and sexism were much more strongly related to support for

Trump," they concluded. "These attitudes [on gender and race] explain at least two-thirds of the education gap among white voters in the 2016 presidential election."

Another important paper, published in 2022, studied "rural consciousness" among white voters outside of urban areas—the heart of the modern Republican Party's coalition. Basically, the researchers were trying to see whether rural voters thought of themselves as a kind of identity group and, if so, how that identity affected their political worldview. The study found that many rural voters indeed believed themselves to be marginalized by the American political mainstream, and that this feeling was strongly associated with support for Trump. However, Trump support was disproportionately concentrated among rural voters who felt marginalized because of "symbolic" concerns—that is, concern over a culture that didn't reflect their communities' beliefs and values. By contrast, voters who felt economically marginalized—that their communities were impoverished and lacking resources—were actually *less* likely to support Trump than the average rural voter.

There are similar findings when you look beyond the Trump question specifically. Political scientist Alan Abramowitz, for example, tracked changes in party identification between 1980 and 2020. Over this forty-year period, his data showed that whites in general (and whites without college degrees in particular) became much more likely to identify with the Republican Party. This was driven primarily by whites who expressed high levels of racial and cultural resentment, with little evidence of economic marginalization playing much of a role. "Among non-college whites," Abramowitz found, "those with lower incomes were actually somewhat less likely to identify as Republicans than those with higher incomes."

Does all this evidence mean that economic inequality is entirely irrelevant to the rise of the reactionary spirit? No, it does not.

In a 2021 paper, Harvard economist Dani Rodrik examined a series of studies tracing the impact of rising trade with China on support for far-right parties and candidates in Europe and the US, and found real evidence that the dislocation of local industry improved the far right's support in affected areas. While not central to the rise of reactionary politics, these effects can matter on the margins (especially in close elections).

More importantly, rising inequality concentrates wealth in the hands of a few people with a vested interest in supporting the status quo distribution of wealth and power. While some of the world's ultrawealthy are left wing, like George Soros and Warren Buffett, research on the top 1 percent suggests that the majority are overwhelmingly opposed to redistributive taxation and thus generally aligned with right-wing factions. Given the disproportionate amount of political influence that can be purchased with tens or hundreds of millions of dollars, just a handful of superwealthy patrons can make a huge impact on the reactionary right's political fortunes.

In *Let Them Eat Tweets*, political scientists Jacob Hacker and Paul Pierson argue that this is a centrally important dynamic in the United States, where America's ultrawealthy see the Republican Party as the key vehicle for keeping taxes low and regulation light. Unfortunately for them, these economic policies are unpopular. In response, economic elites back the GOP's use of culture-war messaging, and sometimes even antidemocratic extremism, as a tool for winning over the masses and enabling the enactment of their "real" agenda.

Whether the global superwealthy are using antidemocratic movements instrumentally in this fashion or they are genuine reactionaries, there's no doubt that the superwealthy have played a powerful role in helping extremist parties succeed. In Israel, the late American businessman Sheldon Adelson created an entire newspaper with a slavishly pro-Likud line—and gave it out for free to ensure that the propaganda spread far and wide. In India, disgraced billionaire Gautam Adani was so close to Prime Minister Narendra Modi that Modi flew on one of Adani's jets after his 2014 electoral victory. And in Hungary, Orbán's government has cultivated a client class of elites who owe their fortunes to the regime's patronage—and thus who willingly serve as a useful means of helping Orbán's party control society without having to exercise an obviously heavy hand.

The theory of the reactionary spirit, in short, does not dismiss the importance of economic factors in shaping the modern rise of the antidemocratic right. Instead, it argues that observers have prioritized the wrong economic explanations.

CHAPTER 4

THE HUNGARIAN MODEL

The Hungarian businessman insisted that I keep his name secret. He was making plans to leave the country but wasn't quite ready. And he was worried that something bad might happen if the government traced my reporting back to him.

We were talking in his office in Budapest, Hungary's beautiful capital city, in the summer of 2018. The place was filled with packing boxes because his company had just been sold. The sale hadn't been voluntary: this businessman had been shaken down, mafia-like, by agents of the Hungarian government.

Some time prior to our meeting, he had received a call from a government official whose work had nothing to do with the man's business (the nature of which I agreed not to disclose, for his safety). The official had allegedly "heard" that the business was up for sale, which was news to the owner, who had never publicly expressed any desire to sell. But after that call, he knew what would happen if he didn't: relentless harassment from regulatory investigations and phony audits until his business was driven into the ground. So he did what any reasonable person would do under the circumstances and sold.

"Anybody who has a conflict with any of [Prime Minister Viktor Orbán's] boys, they will get the tax agency within weeks—for many weeks," he said. "We weren't forced to sell. We just weren't allowed to win."

Before arriving in Hungary, I had expected to be reporting on a troubled democracy. Pretty quickly, I realized the story was much grimmer than that. Hungary was a country where democracy had quietly died—indeed had been murdered. And Prime Minister Orbán was the killer. The outstanding question was the murder weapon: How did he manage to do it in the heart of Europe without many people in Hungary or nearly anybody elsewhere noticing?

My meeting with the businessman was revelatory. It demonstrated that everything in Hungary's state apparatus had been politicized—twisted, generally out of sight and in subtle ways, in service of the interests of the prime minister and his allies. Those interests included staying in power indefinitely and amassing fortunes. They have excelled at both.

Viktor Orbán's Fidesz party has won the past four elections in Hungary, securing a two-thirds majority in parliament every time—but only the first election could be considered remotely fair. Since 2010, Hungary's highest court and its national elections agency have become fully dominated by Fidesz partisans. The party receives a huge advantage through manipulations of election law and campaign-finance regulations, and it even twists Hungary's welfare system to push low-income voters into its corner. By one estimate, 90 percent of Hungarian media is controlled by either the government or a government ally—including every single newspaper in the rural areas, where Fidesz's base resides.

Hungary's richest man is Lőrinc Mészarós, a gas technician by training and a childhood friend of Orbán's. Mészarós, who was not especially wealthy before Orbán's rise to power, is now worth about a billion dollars—a fortune amassed in large part due to government contracts. According to Direkt36, an independent Hungarian media outlet, Mészarós regularly funnels cash to the prime minister's family through publicly funded projects like sewer construction. The term "mafia state," often thrown around by Orbán's critics, is not entirely inaccurate.

The glue that holds Hungary's kleptocratic authoritarian machine together is Orbán's expert manipulation of the reactionary spirit. He has developed an authoritarian system that legitimizes itself through relentless attacks on Schmittian "enemies" of the homogeneously defined Hungarian people—be they migrants, the LGBT community, or the Jewish philanthropist George Soros. This bare-knuckle politics was not something Hungarians were crying out for before 2010. During his time in power, the prime minister has successfully identified fault lines in Hungarian society and hammered them relentlessly, essentially *manufacturing* a sense of threat to existing social hierarchies.

Today, the battle against the global cultural left is his regime's raison d'être, the public-facing justification for his endless efforts to seize tighter control over Hungary's political system, economy, and society. In the Orbánist narrative, liberalism is not merely in tension with democracy but its enemy. Everything Orbán does is in service of protecting his people from the globalist threat against their self-determination. "We do not want to become peoples of mixed-race," he declared in a 2022 speech. "Migration has split Europe in two—or I could say that it has split the West in two. One half is a world where European and non-European peoples live together. These countries are no longer nations: they are nothing more than a conglomeration of peoples."

Orbán has built the perfect authoritarian state for harnessing the reactionary spirit: a legalistic, almost invisibly authoritarian regime seen by its supporters as the last true bulwark of European democracy. This system is so compelling to a certain kind of reactionary that it has amassed a legion of fans outside Hungary's borders—most notably in the United States.

In 2022, Donald Trump endorsed Orbán's fourth consecutive bid for the premiership, praising him as "a strong leader" who has "done a powerful and wonderful job in protecting Hungary." That same year, Orbán was the featured speaker at a CPAC conference in Dallas and his government the subject of a fawning Tucker Carlson special on Fox News. Today he is quite possibly the most popular foreign leader among the American conservative movement.

Ironically, Hungary is now exporting America's own traditional authoritarian style back to the United States—in packaging so slick that many Americans don't grasp what's happening. Hungary is a case study in how the reactionary spirit infects democracy in a thoroughly democratic age—and what happens when the infection becomes terminal.

HOW VIKTOR ORBÁN BUILT HIS REACTIONARY REGIME

The history of the rise of Hungarian authoritarianism is in many ways the history of Viktor Orbán's political ascent. His personal evolution from democrat to dictator mirrors that of the country as a whole.

In 1988, the young Orbán was studying law at the Bibó István College for Advanced Studies. He opposed the existing communist regime, founding Fidesz as a youth political movement with some of his friends. Fidesz would soon emerge as a leading voice of rising anticommunist sentiment; Orbán personally participated in the roundtable talks in 1989 that would eventually lead to a negotiated transition to democracy and a market economy. His profile rose further in June 1989 when, at an event commemorating the 1956 Hungarian uprising against communism, he gave a fiery speech calling for democracy and the withdrawal of Soviet troops from Hungarian territory.

After the communist regime formally fell, Fidesz competed in the country's first elections as a centrist party. Orbán won a seat in parliament and led the party's delegation; he formalized his control over Fidesz in 1993, when he became president of the party organization, a newly created position.

This would prove a crucial year in Fidesz's evolution. In the run-up to the 1994 elections, Orbán intuited that the party's ideology was not distinctive enough. He looked out at the Hungarian political landscape and saw a void on the center right. So Fidesz was reborn as a culturally conservative faction, a move that caused several, more left-leaning Fidesz parliamentarians to quit the party in protest.

I met one of them, an activist named Zsuzsanna Szelényi, in 2018. Szelényi had been with Fidesz since its dissident beginnings and had served in both parliament and party leadership after the democratic transition. She told me about conversations she'd had with Orbán where he described his decision to change Fidesz's ideology in purely mercenary terms: "He said being a liberal democrat is not good enough. Look around in Europe; liberals are small centrist parties, they cannot really be big powers. It's a left-right divided political arena in Europe, so you are either strong as a social democrat or you are strong as a conservative Christian democrat. Because in Hungary, the social democrat [lane] was filled by the Socialist Party, there was only one option where there was actually a vacuum. So he said, okay, why don't we move there, and he made this big shift."

Despite misgivings from longtime members like Szelényi, Fidesz circa 1994 was still well within the postcommunist democratic mainstream. When the party won its first national election in 1998, there was little sense that the young Prime Minister Orbán would pose any threat to Hungarian democracy.

During this first stint in office, he did not do much to fundamentally alter the nature of the country's political system, his policies resembling those of center-right parties ruling around the same time in other European states. After Fidesz's defeat in the 2002 election, the party handed off power to the rival center-left Socialists.

But while Orbán left peacefully after electoral defeat, he did not do so gracefully. Fidesz politicians repeatedly groused about election fraud, even though international observers had generally assessed the vote to be free and fair. The former prime minister complained that the Hungarian press was biased against him and that his party would need to build a more pliant media the next time around.

During his time out of power, Orbán seemed to become more and more comfortable with antidemocratic politics. At a 2009 Fidesz party meeting, he gave a now infamous address where he called for the creation of a "central political force-field" that would be capable of governing the country for up to twenty years. At that point, the party was organizationally the strongest in Hungary, better positioned to compete for votes than any of its rivals. But its once-vibrant internal political culture, which dynamic politicians like Szelényi had formerly found inviting, had long since died—replaced with a near-total subservience to Orbán and his quest for power.

Fidesz would get its chance in 2010, when it won a landslide victory that handed it a two-thirds majority in parliament. This win was not itself powered by the reactionary spirit. The country's economy had been devastated by the 2008 Great Recession; at the same time, the incumbent Socialist government was mired in scandal. Its leader, Ferenc Gyurcsány, had been caught on tape admitting that he had lied about Hungary's economic situation.

Hungarians voted for a democratic change, not an end to democracy. But that's soon what they got. Orbán and his allies approached the construction of an autocratic state like lawyers, altering the Hungarian constitution and legal code in ways both bold and devious. Oftentimes, their approaches were so legally subtle as to be invisible to all but the most attentive experts and activists. Over time, these changes made it harder and harder to dislodge Fidesz through electoral means.

After the 2010 election, Fidesz rewrote the entire Hungarian constitution, a process done in secret. The new constitution passed after only nine days of parliamentary debate. The changes included a restructuring of Hungarian elections, which now determined over half of representatives through single-member, American-style districts (the remainder were determined by a national proportional vote share). In drawing the new districts, Fidesz abused a rule that allowed the government to vary the districts in size between roughly sixty thousand and ninety thousand people. In the new map, opposition voters were packed in a handful of larger districts, diluting their votes, while pro-Fidesz voters were efficiently distributed around smaller ones. The effect was an extreme gerrymander paralleling what was going on in some US states at about the same time. Under the new system, Fidesz could fall short of a popular-vote majority and still win a two-thirds majority in parliament—which happened not once but twice, in the 2014 and 2018 elections.

Fidesz paired these gerrymandered districts with a blizzard of other electoral changes. Each was incremental, potentially even defensible in isolation. But in combination, the laws worked to create extraordinary barriers to opposition parties winning elections. For example, the old system had allowed for a run-off in any individual district if the winning candidate got less than 50 percent of the vote. The new system abolished the run-off, allowing a party to win a district with a mere plurality. At the same time, Fidesz created a rule that required national parties to compete in at least twenty-seven single-member districts—meaning that the various opposition parties were basically forced to split the anti-Fidesz vote in many districts.

This kind of election-law minutiae can be confusing, even boring—and for Fidesz, that was the point. Orbán and his allies used the arcane nature of law as a smokescreen, allowing them to hide the way their new policies entrenched Fidesz's hold on power. Kim Lane Scheppele, a professor at Princeton who studies Hungarian law, has shown that the relevant changes were sometimes hidden across different statutes in unrelated areas. A significant change to election law might end up in, for example, counterterrorism legislation.

Scheppele terms Orbán's overall strategy "autocratic legalism," which she defines as the use of legally aboveboard methods to replace Hungarian democracy with an authoritarian state in an incremental and procedurally sound fashion. Fidesz favors making change through law, especially passing laws that somewhat resemble those in peer democracies, because it allows the party to maintain a democratic veneer—to plausibly say they're standing up for freedom while restricting it.

Understanding this pattern helps expose the insidious logic animating several of Orbán's early policies. A new law lowering the maximum retirement age for judges, from seventy to sixty-two, immediately created hundreds of vacancies that were promptly filled with Fidesz allies. Similarly, Orbán expanded the jurisdiction of the constitutional court, which is tasked with reviewing legislation, creating a huge new caseload for new judges who, again, were reliable Fidesz allies. Later, Orbán would entrench his control over the court even further, forming an entire new court system in 2018 to oversee "administrative" areas like election law and corruption. The new judges were—unsurprisingly—Fidesz cronies.

The party's two-thirds majority in parliament, combined with control over the courts, allowed the government to assert its will across Hungarian society, systematically taking control over institutions that could potentially threaten its lock on political power.

The press was perhaps the most striking example. After the 2010 election, the new government passed a law that brought Hungary's public media outlets, its equivalents of the BBC, under the aegis of a new Fidesz-controlled institution that fired independent reporters and replaced them with government mouthpieces. The new law also created the Media Council, another Fidesz-dominated body, and gave it powers to fine private media organizations for a series of vague offenses like failing to be balanced. According to Marius Dragomir, a professor at Central European University, Orbán sold this move as a "corrective" to left-wing bias in Hungarian media. In reality, "left-wing" meant "independent from Orbán."

But Fidesz's most effective tool in bringing the press to heel may have been simple market pressure. During the 2010s, media globally experienced a revenue crisis thanks to online giants like Google hoovering up advertising dollars. Hungarian media specifically was especially dependent on the government purchasing ads for things like public service announcements. Fidesz politicized this funding stream, shoveling government ad dollars toward friendly outlets while letting critical ones starve until they sold to the state or one of its allies. Whenever this market pressure wasn't enough, the party would use the tools provided by the 2010 media law.

Dragomir's research found that by 2017, roughly 90 percent of all media in Hungary was controlled by the government or one of its allies. On a single day in 2018, Fidesz cronies consolidated around five hundred outlets under the management of a new Fidesz-run "nonprofit" called the Central European Press and Media Foundation, which overnight became the largest media conglomerate in Europe. In 2020, Index—the largest remaining independent outlet in the country—was sold to Fidesz interests. In 2021, the radio station Klubrádió, which had somehow survived losing 90 percent of its ad revenues during Fidesz's first year back in power, was forced off the airwaves by the Media Council. Klubrádió now broadcasts exclusively online; the government gave its former frequency to a pro-Fidesz outlet.

Orbán used similar tactics to bring the business world to heel. Under Fidesz, the Hungarian economy was restructured along political lines; major government contracts went disproportionately to party allies in the private sector, often with little transparent bidding. European Union subsidies provided to support poorer EU countries were now regularly funneled directly into friendly pockets. These practices not only enriched Orbán and his allies personally, but also created a situation where even the superrich would be hard pressed to dissent from the government line.

The fate of Lajos Simicska, a fallen Hungarian oligarch, is instructive. An old-guard Fidesz loyalist, and a personal friend of Orbán's since high school, Simicska became one of the country's wealthiest men after the 2010 election, amassing an empire spanning everything from construction to media to advertising. But in 2014, Simicska and Orbán had a nasty falling out over differing plans for the expansion of Simicska's holdings. The following year, he publicly called the prime minister "*geci*," a Hungarian insult that literally translates to "semen," and instantly became the most influential Fidesz opponent in Hungarian politics. During the 2018 election, he lavished the far-right opposition party Jobbik with funding in a desperate bid to unseat a government he by then was calling a "dictatorship."

Orbán crushed him. By redirecting government support away from Simicska-held corporations, Orbán kneecapped their business model. Simicska rapidly tumbled down the rankings of wealthiest Hungarians. After Fidesz won the 2018 election, Simicska recognized that he had lost. He shut down the remainder of his empire or sold it to progovernment interests. Simicska is now a nonfactor in Hungarian politics.

Fidesz's comprehensive control over government and private power centers means that Hungary is in the grips of a near-perfect competitive authoritarian regime. Elections do not need to be nakedly rigged, in the sense of falsified vote counts, because the deck is so stacked against the opposition that winning is functionally impossible. The greatest proof of the system's resilience came in 2022, when Hungary's main opposition parties united on a single ticket. In each district, these combined parties carefully selected candidates—more conservative ones in rural areas, more left-leaning ones in Budapest—who would best compete with Fidesz. The idea was to circumvent the system that had forced vote splitting between opposition candidates and give the Hungarian people a binary choice: Fidesz or literally anyone else.

Perhaps this gambit could have worked in 2014, before Orbán had fully consolidated control. But in the intervening years, the electoral rules and the press had become so tilted that even a united opposition faced nearly insurmountable challenges. In 2020, the government had stripped 50 percent of funds from public elections (claiming the money was needed to finance the coronavirus response). This essentially only hurt opposition parties, as Fidesz could rely on private funding and government "public service announcements" to make up the deficit. Blatantly circumventing campaign-spending laws, Fidesz put up nearly eight times as many campaign billboards as the entire opposition combined.

Financially hobbled, fighting on a gerrymandered map, and unable to get their message out given government control of the press, the opposition was crushed. Fidesz won another two-thirds majority in parliament, fueled in large part by victories in single-member districts outside Budapest—where it won an astonishing 98 percent of seats.

Outside Hungary, it was easy to see that the country had crossed the line into competitive authoritarianism. But domestically, Fidesz managed to sustain the fiction of a democratic Hungary for a critical mass of Hungarians. In a 2022 Pew poll, 85 percent of the party's supporters said that Hungary under Orbán was equally democratic as or even more so than it had been before 2010.

These genuine supporters are the linchpin of the entire system. Without a hard-core bloc who genuinely vote for Fidesz, Orbán would have to resort to more naked forms of authoritarianism—like falsifying vote counts and violently repressing dissenters—in order to stay in office. The system works in a self-reinforcing manner: Orbán's supporters hand him power, which he uses to control what his supporters hear and see about politics, which in turn ensures they vote for him again.

Such a system depends on Orbán continuing to give these voters something they want and telling them things they want to hear. So what does the government offer to keep them loyal?

HUNGARY'S MANUFACTURED REACTION

In 2018, after Orbán had just been sworn in as prime minister for the fourth time, he gave a speech in which he grandly pronounced that "the age of liberal democracy is at an end." Attacks on "liberal democracy" had long been a staple of Orbán's rhetoric. According to the Hungarian prime minister, liberalism has slowly been sapping the foundations of European civilization. If left unchecked, he argued, it would lead to the destruction of what makes Europe truly European. "Liberal democracy is no longer able to protect people's dignity, provide freedom, guarantee physical security or maintain Christian culture," he said in the 2018 address. "Our response to this changed world, the Hungarian people's response, has been to replace the shipwreck of liberal democracy."

Orbán refers to his replacement system as "illiberal democracy" or, less threateningly, "Christian democracy." Though it's obvious to any clear-eyed observer outside Hungary that it is no democracy at all, Orbán needs to convince both his own supporters and ideological sympathizers abroad that he remains within the democratic family. So to maintain the veneer of democracy while undermining it from within, he has deployed Carl Schmitt's old playbook: pitting liberalism against democracy and claiming to stand in defense of the latter against the former. As long as attacks on essential democratic rights and freedoms can be described as attacks on "liberalism," a defense of nationalist and conservative values against an encroaching liberal tide, he can credibly claim that some of his efforts to undermine Hungarian democracy are actually intended to preserve it.

This strategy works by ginning up the reactionary spirit. Through demagogic appeals to an especially conservative segment of the Hungarian population, one discomfited by the politics of equality at the heart of modern democracy, he can tap into social conservatism to support Fidesz's assaults on liberal-democratic institutions.

Unlike in the United States, where Obama's victory triggered a wave of reactionary sentiment among the GOP grassroots and rank-and-file operatives, it does not appear as if any new developments lit a fire under the Hungarian public overnight. Some events—most notably the 2015 refugee crisis—played a crucial role in the reactionary spirit's surge, but it would be wrong to say that the Hungarian people revolted from the bottom up once migrants began streaming across their country's southern border.

Rather, reactionary sentiment was heavily manufactured, the result of Fidesz working extensively over the course of years to stoke public concern about a declining West and a global plot against Hungary. The prime minister's rhetoric and the progovernment media painted a picture of nefarious international liberals corrupting everything Hungarian conservatives held dear, an existential threat that justified Fidesz's illiberal politics. The citizens of Hungary did not organically come to believe that democratic rights posed a threat to the existing social order; they were convinced by a political faction that had been searching for a way to justify its own authoritarianism.

Elements of this strategy were visible as early as Orbán's first term. In a 2000 essay in the *Boston Review*, leading Hungarian philosopher G. M. Tamás warned that the prime minister represented the ideological vanguard of a political tendency that he termed "post-fascism."

Tamás and Orbán were once allies; by 2000, however, Tamás had come to see Orbán as an enemy of Hungary, warning that his government was "creating and imposing a novel state ideology, with the help of a number of *lumpen* intellectuals of the extreme right, including some overt neo-Nazis."

In its conservative iteration, Fidesz's rhetoric had become intensely nationalistic, focusing on the post–World War I Treaty of Trianon, which had stripped Hungary of some of its lands and stranded hundreds of thousands of ethnic Hungarians outside the country's borders. Fidesz's pan-Hungarian rhetoric, according to Tamás, ended up describing the nation in purely ethnic terms, suggesting that "citizens of their nation-state who are ethnically, racially, denominationally, or culturally 'alien' do not really belong to the nation."

At the time, Tamás's views must have seemed alarmist given Fidesz's relatively unthreatening policy agenda. But his charge of "post-fascism" correctly identified the Schmittian core of Orbán's new politics. Long before almost anyone else, Tamás grasped that the friend/enemy distinction was becoming central to the government's approach to politics—and that this politics could provide a kind of legitimacy to outright antidemocratic moves.

This is not the politics that powered Fidesz's next electoral victory, in 2010, a campaign that was primarily fought on the grounds of economics and corruption. But once Orbán took his mandate and began rewriting the constitution, he needed some way to legitimize power grabs that had nothing to do with his campaign platform. For that, he turned to the Schmittian politics of friend and enemy.

During the 2010 campaign, Orbán worked with a pair of American political consultants—Arthur Finkelstein and George Birnbaum—at the recommendation of a friend, Israeli prime minister Benjamin Netanyahu. Finkelstein in particular was known in the US as a master of negative campaigning; Birnbaum was his deputy and protégé. When it came time to prepare for Orbán's 2014 reelection bid, the two men realized they needed to use a similar playbook to secure victory. So Birnbaum and Finkelstein set out to find someone who could personally exemplify the liberal-cosmopolitan evils that Orbán railed against. They picked George Soros, a Hungarian-born American billionaire and Holocaust survivor.

Soros had long been the principal funder of prodemocracy civil society groups in Hungary, both before and after the fall of the communist regime. During Orbán's anticommunist dissident days, he used a copy machine purchased with Soros cash to distribute a newspaper, and he received a "Soros scholarship" to study at Oxford from 1989 to 1990. Orbán, who according to Birnbaum had "an enormous amount of trust" in Finkelstein's judgment, supported their choice of Soros as public enemy number one. Beginning around 2013, Fidesz and its aligned media institutions began attacking the philanthropist as a menace to ordinary Hungarians.

It was an inspired choice. Because Soros had been such a generous donor, it was easy to point to the large number of

Hungarian institutions receiving his money as evidence that he was manipulating the country from behind the scenes. And because his dollars had gone to both prodemocracy and socially liberal groups, it became easy for Orbán to tie the two together. He painted the entire spectrum of Hungarian civil society institutions, human rights groups, and scholars who called out his antidemocratic behavior as part of the "Soros-funded" plot against traditional Hungary. The scheme allowed him to mount attacks on core elements of Hungarian democracy in the name of fighting Sorosian liberalism—and to get millions of Hungarians to cheer him on while doing it. By 2014, the war on Hungarian civil society had gotten so intense that President Barack Obama publicly compared Orbán's crackdown with one imposed by authoritarian Egypt.

The following year's refugee crisis was a political gift to Orbán's reactionary PR campaign. While very few refugees attempted to settle in Hungary, hundreds of thousands attempted to pass through it. Geographically, Hungary is at the southeastern edge of the European Union, which meant that Syrian refugees journeying either overland through Turkey or across the Mediterranean Sea to Greece often traveled through Hungary on their way to Germany or other EU member states. About 391,000 refugees entered Hungary in the summer of 2015 alone. Budapest's Keleti train station turned into a functional refugee camp as hundreds of migrants waited at any given time to depart to Austria, Czechia, or Germany.

There's no doubt that the refugee influx was majorly disruptive for many Hungarians—and in the chaos, Orbán saw political opportunity. In the prime minister's speeches, government statements, and relentless coverage in state-run media, the same message was repeated over and over again: if migration was allowed to continue, then Hungary and all of

Europe would cease to exist. It was not a humanitarian crisis, but a kind of invasion. "What is at stake today is Europe and the European way of life, the survival or extinction of European values and nations," Orbán said in a 2015 address. "We want to preserve Hungary as a Hungarian country."

Orbán's argument was first and foremost a demographic one. Migrants from non-European countries had different cultural and racial backgrounds, he claimed, and therefore would alter Europe beyond any recognition. "Immigration . . . upsets the balance of the continent. It implants among us a culture and an outlook on life with a mentality and customs which are completely different from ours," he said.

The government's line frequently veered into conspiracy theory. Fidesz and its captive press argued that the refugee crisis was not a tragedy caused by wars around the globe, but one component of a nefarious plot masterminded by—who else?— George Soros: an intentional effort to replace native-born white Europeans with a very different kind of person and culture. "Those who do not halt immigration at their borders are lost: slowly but surely they are consumed. External forces and international powers want to force all this upon us, with the help of their allies here in our country," Orban declared in a 2018 speech. "We are up against media outlets maintained by foreign concerns and domestic oligarchs, professional hired activists, troublemaking protest organizers, and a chain of NGOs financed by an international speculator, summed up by and embodied in the name George Soros."

With this line, Orbán had discovered a powerful way to inflame a sense of cultural threat among the Hungarian population. His government had taken a very real problem, a mass influx of refugees, and rearticulated it as an existential threat to the Hungarian social hierarchy and way of life.

The mastermind behind these events, a Jewish billionaire, was motivated by "liberal" notions of equality and universal humanity—and it was this liberalism, according to Orbán, that underpinned the migrant assault on the foundations of Hungarian and European culture.

Polling data showed that Orbán's attacks resonated. In fall 2015, a Eurobarometer survey indicated that Hungary was the only country in the European Union where an outright majority said they felt "very negative" about immigration from outside the EU.

"The central Fidesz claim [in the 2018 election] was that Brussels and Soros were scheming to flood Europe with Muslim migrants, and that a Fidesz loss would mean the doom of white, Christian Hungary," Hungarian scholars Péter Krekó and Zsolt Enyedi wrote in the *Journal of Democracy*. "This campaign strongly succeeded. Before the refugee crisis, Fidesz's popularity was on the decline. After it, Fidesz not only recovered but added half a million new voters."

The Soros-migrant attack was not merely a means of boosting Fidesz's poll numbers; it also served as a Trojan horse to extend the party's control over Hungarian society. Time and time again, the government would propose a bill that would limit the rights of Hungarian institutions that opposed state ideology or would outright ban them—and justify such measures by the need to fight the conspiracy against the Hungarian nation.

One of the most striking examples is a 2018 law that made it a crime to help undocumented refugees. The government called it the "Stop Soros" law and billed it as an explicit response to his alleged conspiracy against the Hungarian people. In practice, it was so broadly worded—prohibiting anyone from "promoting and supporting illegal migration"—that it threatened

122 | THE REACTIONARY SPIRIT

to criminalize routine activities of Hungarian human rights groups. Shortly afterward, the government passed another law that levied a 25 percent tax on any organization that advocated for migration, legal or otherwise.

The burden was so onerous that Central European University, the leading social science university in Hungary, was forced to shut down its program that provided education to migrants. CEU, founded by Soros in 1991 to educate Hungarians in the ideas that underpinned democracy, would be forced to leave Hungary altogether in a matter of months, the result of a lengthy government campaign of legislative and regulatory harassment.

During the refugee crisis, Orbán brilliantly manipulated events to inflame Hungary's reactionary spirit, using the power of his new authoritarian state to stoke reactionary panic. The ultimate aim was polarizing the Hungarian public against some of democracy's core institutions. It was the perfect variant of the reactionary spirit for the modern age, one that allowed him to erode democracy in a manner invisible to the ordinary voters who played an important part in his scheme.

Fidesz's Schmittian politics has proven quite adaptable. As memories of the refugee crisis faded by the end of the 2010s, the Fidesz party had to find a new cultural enemy. Like other factions globally, it alighted on the LGBT community. The attacks drew from the same ideological well as the attacks on migrants, positioning what Orbán calls "gender ideology" as a demographic threat that had been imported by foreigners. The foreign proponents of gender ideology, according to Fidesz propaganda, were working to turn Hungarian children gay—and thus undermine Hungary's ability to replace itself with native-born children.

"The Western Left attack the traditional family model, first of all, by relativising the concept of the family. The LGBTQ lobby and gender propaganda are all part of this. They specifically target our children, and so we must defend ourselves," the prime minister said in a September 2021 speech at a demography conference.

Several months before that address, Fidesz passed a new law that showed what "defending ourselves" really meant. K–12 schools were banned from teaching about LGBT sexuality. Advertisers couldn't include queer themes in any publication marketed to individuals under eighteen. Television stations were no longer permitted to air shows that "popularized" LGBT identity outside the hours of ten p.m. to five a.m. These moves created new tools that the government could use to control what information the public saw and heard. The goal was not only to demonize the LGBT community but also more broadly cement Fidesz's power over Hungarian minds. In a country dominated by the reactionary spirit, the line between illiberal and antidemocratic can be nonexistent.

The evidence suggests that the demonization of out-groups has been effective: that deep cultural divisions stoked by the government are, fundamentally, at the heart of Fidesz's appeal among its base. In 2022, Pew's survey found that 70 percent of those age sixty-five and older approved of Orbán's performance—compared with just 45 percent of those between eighteen and twenty-nine. The rural-urban split is nearly identical: 69 percent of rural Hungarians support Orbán, while only 44 percent of city dwellers do.

These patterns are difficult to explain in class terms. Although it's true that Fidesz does disproportionately well with the poor and working class, that effect is heavily mediated by location: a poor voter in Budapest is much less likely to support

Fidesz than one outside the capital. Moreover, the wealthy have gained far more than the poor during the party's rule. A 2020 European Commission report found that real income gains in Hungary have been concentrated among the country's top 1 percent, while the incomes of the poor have grown far less rapidly. This is unusual when compared with Hungary's peers: an average of the other countries in the Visegrad Group (Poland, Czechia, and Slovakia) shows the poor gaining considerably more in percentage terms than the rich.

If class is not a good explanation for the demographics of Fidesz's appeal, ideology and identity fit the bill better. Across Western democracies, rural voters without college degrees tend to have the most culturally conservative views about issues like immigration and LGBT rights. The countryside—with weaker internet access, less frequent experience with foreigners, and a local media landscape utterly dominated by government-friendly outlets—is also where Fidesz's control is most absolute. Furthermore, Fidesz's political control creates more overt mechanisms of political control. There's evidence that Fidesz mayors in small towns condition employment in public works projects on their employees voting for the ruling party.

Economic factors are also relevant. A 2020 paper by five Hungarian political scientists examined the voting patterns of the poor and socially marginalized specifically, and found that those who evaluated the economic situation more favorably were considerably more likely to vote for Fidesz than those who didn't. Indeed, Fidesz often introduces expanded economic benefits in the immediate run-up to elections; in 2022, the party hiked pension payments for seniors and eliminated the income tax for Hungarians under twenty-five.

But the paper also found considerable evidence that the poor were manipulated, through economic coercion at the local level and through government media, to support the ruling party. And when you look at what Fidesz's rich and poor voters have in common, the through line is typically some kind of ideological agreement with the government's worldview. "Previous studies have shown that [support for Fidesz] is mainly due to ideological reasons," the researchers wrote.

Orbán has built a deep reservoir of authentic support for his party's reactionary ideology among Hungary's older and rural voters—a base that not only allows Fidesz to run a kleptocratic economy, but also enables attacks on democracy in the name of defending Hungary from liberalism.

HOW HUNGARY IS EXPORTING ITS MODEL TO THE UNITED STATES—AND BEYOND

In April 2022, I came across a surprising claim: that Florida's new "Don't Say Gay" law restricting LGBT education in public schools was literally patterned after similar regulations Hungary had passed a year prior.

When I asked Governor Ron DeSantis's press secretary Christina Pushaw about the connection, she initially denied it. But then a Hungarian source pointed me to some interesting comments from Rod Dreher, a conservative American writer. Dreher had emerged as one of the biggest Orbán boosters on the American right; he was so dedicated, in fact, that he eventually moved to Hungary for a job at a government-funded think tank called the Danube Institute. During a panel talk in Budapest, Dreher said the laws were indeed related—and cited Pushaw as his ultimate source.

"About the Don't Say Gay law, it was in fact modeled in part on what Hungary did last summer," Dreher said. "I was told this by a conservative reporter who . . . said he talked to the press secretary of Governor Ron DeSantis of Florida, and she said, 'Oh yeah, we were watching the Hungarians, so yay Hungary.'"

Dreher, it seemed, had accidentally spilled the beans: one of the Republican Party's rising stars was taking notes from the European Union's only authoritarian regime.

When I first went to Hungary in 2018, there were no such hints of direct ties between Fidesz and the GOP. Orbán was a nonentity in Republican politics; the idea that he might directly influence one of the party's most important governors would have been largely unthinkable. But over the course of the next few years, the radicalizing American right fell in love with Orbán's Hungary. By 2022, it had become to the American right what the Nordic countries have long been to the American left: a utopian blueprint for what their country could and should be.

This was a major policy victory for Orbán, who has spent millions on lobbyists and organizations like the Danube Institute to make Fidesz's case to a global audience. But many countries spend lavishly on public relations and foreign lobbying without winning the heart of one of the two major parties in the world's only superpower. Hungary's rise in America is not just about money; it is a reflection of a deep ideological affinity between Fidesz and the GOP.

On a policy level, what's happened in Hungary can be seen as an updating and refining of the American authoritarian tradition. The legal tactics Fidesz uses to maintain power are not dissimilar from some used in the Jim Crow South and in today's most ruthless Republican-run states. They are, however, considerably more subtle than the former and more aggressive than anything that exists in the latter. Hungary has built a blueprint for a twenty-first-century authoritarian state that effectively masquerades as a democracy. There's something ironic about the fact that it's now exporting its ideology and tactics to the country where this form of reactionary authoritarianism was born.

But there's also a broader lesson about the reactionary spirit and its global rise. The American right's affection for Hungary shows how the reactionary spirit's family resemblance to regular conservatism, visible in their shared commitment to preserving existing social arrangements, is critical to reactionary flourishing in democracies nominally dedicated to equality.

When you read Hungary's admirers in the American press, they insist that Hungary remains a democracy. Hungary is a model not of authoritarianism, according to these commentators, but of effective Christian conservative governance. "I find myself saying of Orbán what I hear conservatives say when they explain why they instinctively love Trump: because he fights," Dreher told me over email in 2020. "The thing about Orbán is that unlike Trump, he fights, and he wins, and his victories are substantive."

This is mostly right. Orbán has indeed won a string of victories in the culture war, an increasingly central preoccupation of conservative parties around the world. He has banned gay couples from adopting, built a barrier on the Serbian border to block migration, and barred government IDs from recognizing a person's gender as anything other than the one assigned at birth. Hungary's education system is dominated by the right; so, too, is its mainstream media. Hungarian conservatives have won the culture war in a way that its peers haven't anywhere else in the Western world. It's easy to see why some on the global right would find something to admire, even envy, in those accomplishments.

But Orbán is not a normal conservative. He is an authoritarian who, to secure his hold on power, has evolved into a living embodiment of the reactionary spirit. He has self-consciously instrumentalized a central component of conservatism, its commitment to seeing value in tradition and existing social norms, in service of an authoritarian and kleptocratic agenda. To acknowledge this reality would make it impossible for conservatives who claim to stand for democratic ideals to celebrate Hungary in any real sense.

The simple solution to this problem is denial: to repeatedly and loudly insist that Hungarian elections are still free, that its press remains independent, that its civil society remains vibrant. If reporters and academics call Hungary "authoritarian," they can be easily dismissed as cultural liberals who oppose its cultural politics. Hence a proliferation of voices that not only are outright supporters of Orbán, like Dreher, but also take a sort of anti-anti-Orbán stance: conservatives who may not directly praise Orbán but repeatedly and harshly denounce his critics. "One suspects [that allegations of authoritarianism are] just simple hatred of Christian conservatism, a fanatical projection of culture war antipathies to the near abroad," the journalist Michael Brendan Dougherty, one such anti-anti-Orbán voice, wrote in *National Review*.

Of course, there is nothing uniquely conservative about idealizing foreign autocrats. Some of the leading lights of the Western left routinely exaggerated the Soviet Union's accomplishments and downplayed its crimes, even at the height of Stalinist depravity. One of history's most influential libertarian thinkers, the economist Friedrich Hayek, repeatedly defended

Augusto Pinochet's murderous dictatorship in Chile on anti-socialist grounds.

But the modern manifestation of the reactionary spirit, disguised in democratic language and concepts, makes authoritarian envy on the contemporary right especially dangerous. There was never any risk that a Soviet apologist might win a national election in Cold War America; no libertarian politician won power on a platform of instituting a Pinochet-style dictatorship in Western Europe. A platform of outright democratic rejection doesn't work in a context where democracy represents the consensus position.

Yet Donald Trump is an open Orbán admirer. So are Ron DeSantis and many other leading Republicans. Orbán's authoritarian legalism is designed to create the appearance of democracy, and it does so well enough that those inclined to agree with him have some plausible deniability about celebrating an authoritarian leader.

This is what makes Hungary's effort to export its model so dangerous. The reactionary spirit, when it sufficiently masks its authoritarian aspirations, can seem extremely similar to mere cultural conservatism. The resemblance invites even more mainstream conservatives to antidemocratic reactionary politics. The more popular Hungary becomes on the international mainstream right, the more its variant of reactionary authoritarianism influences world politics.

Orbán has, of course, deliberately conflated his hard-line tactics with mainstream conservatism. In his speech to CPAC Dallas, he argued that "we [conservatives] cannot fight successfully by liberal means" because "our opponents use liberal institutions, concepts, and language to disguise their Marxist and hegemonist plans." Liberalism is, per Orbán, not an essential bulwark of democracy but a front for a kind of leftist authoritarianism. Only by rejecting liberalism and destroying its "institutions" can conservatives of any stripe hope to win the culture war. He is not persuading the right to abandon democracy outright, but rather seducing them—telling them they have no choice but to fight dirty, "illiberally," if they want to beat back the left. Since he's broadly on their team, railing against their shared enemies, the CPAC audience was willing to listen.

For over a decade after the 2010 election, Fidesz remained a member of the European People's Party—a faction of the European Parliament for center-right parties that includes (for example) Germany's Christian Democrats. During that time, Hungary's membership in the EPP repeatedly shielded it from efforts to use the European Union's powers to arrest the country's antidemocratic drift.

Lili Bayer, a Hungary beat reporter currently with *The Guardian*, once wrote that "Orbán broke the EU and got away with it" for precisely this reason. She assembled quote after quote from members of the European Parliament who said that the EPP bloc protected Orbán because he was on their political side. The more anti-immigration members of the EPP in particular saw him as a leader on that issue. During the refugee crisis, they treated attacks on Orbán's democracy record as attempts to punish him for his immigration policy—and rejected them accordingly.

The EPP is not a group of Europe's far-right parties but the umbrella faction for Europe's *center right*, the mainstream parties that are theoretically committed to the European project and its core democratic values. That Orbán managed to dupe the EPP for so long, until he was forced out in 2021, shows how effectively his kind of reactionary politics can damage democratic institutions from within. More aggressive EU actions, most notably a 2022 suspension of subsidies on rule-of-law grounds, have not cowed Hungary. In December 2023, Hungary blocked billions in EU support for Ukraine—a veto that it was prepared to lift, per one top Orbán advisor, if the EU unfroze Hungary's funds. A core objective of the EU, protecting Europe's democratic order, was seemingly held hostage by an autocracy inside the bloc.

Under Orbán, Hungary has become an authoritarian beachhead in the heart of the democratic world—encouraging antidemocratic tendencies on the American right, and weakening the ability of the European Union to defend and promote democracy. His rise shows how the reactionary spirit not merely is growing in different countries because they share certain features in common, but is actively contagious. An outbreak in one place, even a place as small as Hungary, can intensify the global epidemic.

CHAPTER 5

A WARNING FROM JERUSALEM

Givon HaHadasha is, on the surface, a suburb like many others in Israel. Located a little over twenty minutes north of Jerusalem, the town's roughly one thousand residents commute to work on quiet, leafy streets. It's all entirely unremarkable except for one thing: the fenced-in Palestinian home it surrounds.

The Gharib family, who nominally reside in the neighboring Palestinian village of Beit Ijza, had the misfortune of living about 130 feet away from its town center—putting them directly adjacent to Givon HaHadasha. The Israeli town is not only a Jerusalem suburb but also a West Bank settlement, built after Israel took the territory during 1967's Six-Day War. In response to settlers' fears about living so close to Palestinians, Israeli authorities sealed off the Gharib home from those of their Israeli neighbors. The house is hemmed in on three sides by a barbed-wire fence; to get to Beit Ijza, the Gharibs have to walk through a tight corridor that looks like the entrance to a prison. The Israeli settlers move around freely, able to peer in at the Gharibs in their cage.

The contrast is unforgettable: it encapsulates what's really happening in the Israeli-occupied West Bank. The residents of Givon HaHadasha cannot ignore what life is like for West Bank Palestinians in the way that many inside Israel's internationally recognized borders can easily do. Instead, they confront it daily—and somehow go on living as if everything is fine.

I've known Israelis for nearly my entire life; they are not cruel or evil people as a rule. But how could they live with this, seeing such a grotesquerie as part of everyday life? When I visited Givon HaHadasha in 2022, I got so caught up in thinking this through while standing on the street staring at the Gharibs' house through their cage that my travel partner started to get a little nervous.

Yehuda Shaul is a cofounder of Breaking the Silence, a group that compiles testimonies from soldiers who have served in war or in the Israeli-occupied territories. Because the testimonies frequently highlight human rights abuses committed by the Israeli Defense Forces (IDF), the group is very controversial inside Israel. Yehuda and I had met on one of my prior trips to Israel and instantly gotten along, talking late into the night about the conflict and Israel's political future.

Part of Yehuda's work today is leading West Bank tours for journalists like me, educational trips that examine the history and policy behind the Israeli occupation of the West Bank. Some extremist settlers know him on sight—and aim to make his life miserable. At an earlier stop, Yehuda saw one such radical pumping gas; he stayed in the car and slid behind the front seat to avoid a fight. And "fight" is meant literally; in the city of Hebron, where this settler was from, Yehuda had once been punched in the face by an angry right-wing activist. He told me there had been another violent incident on a recent trip to Givon HaHadasha.

Yehuda is not a coward. He served as a combat soldier in the early 2000s, at the height of the Second Intifada, one of the bloodiest episodes of the Israeli-Palestinian conflict. He was worried about his safety, and mine, for good reason. His office has been threatened—Israeli police once arrested a man who had stockpiled accelerants to set the building on fire—and he regularly travels to places full of people who hate him. If he felt that things could get ugly quickly, it was time to leave.

Givon HaHadasha is the physical incarnation of a fundamental Israeli contradiction. Since 1967, the country has attempted to run two parallel forms of government at the same time: a liberal democracy within its internationally recognized borders, and an authoritarian military occupation in the lands largely populated by Palestinians. It has proven impossible to keep them fully separate; the ideas and practices that underpin the occupation and the settlements inescapably clash with the liberal-democratic institutions that govern Israel proper. That tension is at the heart of Israel's reactionary spirit: a conflict between the maintenance of an existing social hierarchy, in this case Jewish supremacy in all the land west of the Jordan River, and democracy's principle of universal equality.

Israel today is not dissimilar to the United States in 1858, when Abraham Lincoln famously claimed that "a house divided against itself cannot stand." Lincoln was referring not only to the deep tension between the North and the South, but also to a deeper legal and political reality. He believed that the legal and political machinery necessary to maintain the slave system would invariably cause slavery to creep outside the South's borders. The future president predicted that "either the opponents of slavery will arrest the further spread of it, and place it where the public mind shall rest in the belief that it is in the course of ultimate extinction; or its *advocates* will push it forward, till it shall become alike lawful in *all* the States." This, he concluded, was why the Union "cannot endure permanently half slave and half free."

Much of Israel's modern history rotates around the question of how its own house divided could be made whole. In the 1990s, and even in a handful of moments in the 2000s, it appeared as if Israel was moving toward a peace agreement with the Palestinians that would bring the occupation to a close. Since then, things have gone in the opposite direction: the laws and values governing the occupation have crept westward, mainstreaming a bevy of undemocratic ideas and corrupting the Israeli political system. This antidemocratic rot explains not only the violence directed at activists like Yehuda Shaul but also a more insidious growth of legal practices designed to trample the rights of Arab Palestinian citizens and silence their Jewish allies. Prime Minister Benjamin Netanyahu, who has been in office longer than any other Israeli leader, has used his power to undermine the freedom of the press, attack the independence of government agencies, and define Arab citizens out of the polity. Most dramatically, he attempted to pass legislation in 2023 imposing political controls over the Supreme Court—a move that was motivated in no small part by the court's fitful attempts to limit West Bank settlement expansion.

The occupation and the settlements are not the only causes of Israel's democratic crisis. Israel has always defined itself as a

"Jewish and democratic state," but there's an inherent tension between these two components of Israeli identity: privileging a particular ethnoreligious group on the one hand, while remaining committed to democracy and its fundamental principle of equality on the other. It is a particularly acute version of the problem inherent to democratic universalism identified by Schmitt a hundred years ago: Who counts as a "Jew," and what should Israel do with those who don't? Conflict over issues related to these questions—like the rights of Arab citizens and the Orthodox Chief Rabbinate's control over key areas of civil law—has contributed mightily to the contemporary rise of Israel's reactionary spirit.

It's tempting to think of Israel as a sui generis case—a nation whose struggles contain few lessons for other countries. Israel, the only Jewish state, was born out of the uniquely Jewish experience of centuries of persecution in Europe, culminating in the Holocaust. It is the only advanced democracy that maintains anything like the occupation of Palestinian land. And it is practically alone in being a rich, developed country that was nearly wiped off the face of the earth several times in post–World War II history. In the fall of 2023, Israel experienced the worst terrorist attack of its history: the October 7 massacre by the Palestinian militant group Hamas, which US president Joe Biden compared in severity to "fifteen 9/11s" given Israel's population relative to America's. Israel responded to the attack by waging a bloody and vicious war to remove Hamas from power in Gaza—killing tens of thousands of Palestinians and turning much of the Strip's houses to rubble.

Can a democracy with such acute security threats really be compared with any other? The answer, in short, is yes.

There are some universal elements of the Israeli predicament—most notably, the way in which fundamental tension between hierarchy and democratic equality has fueled democratic backsliding. Looking at Israel through a global lens can help us better understand how and why its democracy has degraded—the reasons that it looks to be at an earlier stage of the process of institutional decay that took down Hungarian democracy. The comparative lens can also help us make sense of the *resistance* to the backsliding, like the massive street demonstrations—the largest in the country's history—protesting Netanyahu's 2023 attempt to reform the courts.

On the flip side, studying Israel's history also can deepen our understanding of the reactionary spirit's operations in other countries. In particular, Israel shows us how the increasingly popular model of illiberal democracy—a system that remains democratic but lacks meaningful checks and balances that prevent elected governments from sharply restricting the rights of minorities—makes a country inherently vulnerable to outright democratic decay.

Israel illustrates, perhaps better than any other country on the planet, how the fundamental tension between Schmittian illiberalism and democracy opens the door to reactionary backsliding. A democracy defined by sharp distinctions between "friend" and "enemy" is not more stable, as Schmitt's theory implies, but in fact more *vulnerable* to internal conflict over its democratic character. Such instability is inherent to the project of illiberal democracy, which proposes to treat inequality and equality as coequal governing ideals. Israel shows how and why this form of government is not, as Orbán and others have suggested, a viable approach to democracy in the twenty-first century.

THE CRISIS OF "ETHNIC DEMOCRACY"

Like a lot of American Jews, I grew up learning about Israel as a remarkable success story. A country founded in 1948 by former colonial subjects and Holocaust survivors like my grandparents—people who had nothing and came from nothing—survived multiple major wars with neighboring Arab countries in its first three decades. Yet it still chose to grant Arab Muslims inside its borders citizenship and voting rights, integrating them (at least to a limited degree) into Israeli social and cultural life. By the 1990s, when I was in grade school, Israel had become one of the world's wealthiest democracies, having undergone a rapid economic and political rise with few global peers.

This narrative wasn't false, exactly. But it was blinkered. It skipped over the mass expulsions of Palestinians during Israel's 1948 War of Independence, an event Palestinians remember as the Nakba (the catastrophe). It ignored the fact that Palestinian citizens of Israel were governed under martial law until 1966 and remained socially marginalized afterward. Palestinians in the West Bank and Gaza, lands taken in the Six-Day War, were placed under indefinite military rule in 1967, with Israeli settlers, supported by the government, seizing huge chunks of Palestinian-owned land. And that's to say nothing of the inequalities *between* Jews. The European Ashkenazim had long controlled the commanding heights of Israeli society, marginalizing the Middle Eastern Mizrahim. The Orthodox religious establishment controlled the law on civil issues like marriage, to the detriment of basically everyone else.

Both these ways of looking at Israel—as a success story and an oppression story—capture certain aspects of the truth. Yet taken in isolation, they paint a seemingly contradictory picture of Israel's history and democracy. So how can these facts be reconciled? How ought we think about a state that does not fit the conventional model of full liberal democracy but also cannot fairly be described as authoritarian?

Sammy Smooha, an eminent Israeli sociologist, has developed an influential answer: that Israel is best seen as a particular kind of democracy, one he terms an "ethnic democracy." Such a system "combines the extension of civil and political rights to individuals and some collective rights to minorities, with institutionalization of major control over the state. Driven by ethnic nationalism, the state is identified with a 'core ethnic nation' not with its citizens."

In Israeli ethnic democracy, Jewish identity and symbols retain a special status because the purpose of the state is identified with the survival and flourishing of the Jewish people. Jews receive legal privileges in important areas, like immigration, while the Arab Palestinian minority is, according to Smooha, "treated as second-class citizens, feared as a threat, excluded from the national power structure, and placed under some control."

Yet unlike the Jim Crow South or apartheid South Africa, Arab citizens of Israel are also "allowed to conduct a democratic and peaceful struggle that yields incremental improvement in their status." Thus, Smooha concluded, "Ethnic democracy is a system in which two contradictory principles operate: 'the democratic principle,' making for equal rights and equal treatment of all citizens, and 'the ethnic principle,' making for fashioning a homogenous nation-state and privileging the ethnic majority."

This system has faced pressure from all sides. Arab citizens' successful activism on their own behalf has weakened the ethnic components of the state in favor of the democratic ones. So too have the efforts of more left-leaning

Israeli Jews, who have argued for moving toward full Arab civic equality and diminishing the role of religion in public life. By contrast, Orthodox and politically right-wing Jews have worked to enshrine a more aggressive Jewish identity, privileging Jews and specifically the Orthodox religious establishments.

But the leading stressor on Israeli democracy has long been the occupation. Unlike Palestinian citizens of Israel, residents of the West Bank and the Gaza Strip neither had nor wanted any role in the Israeli state—and the Israelis were not inclined to give them one. Such a population could not be assimilated according to the model of ethnic democracy, where Palestinians functioned as a minority with citizens' rights operating within the confines of a Jewish state. They wanted something of their own: a Palestinian state. If Israel continued to allow and even encourage Jewish settlers to move into the territories, living as Israeli citizens next to Palestinians held under military rule, it would cease to be an ethnic democracy in Smooha's sense and become something much more akin to apartheid.

These contradictions at the heart of Israel's project of ethnic democracy have long been evident. In the 1990s, they led to a crisis—specifically, a left-wing effort to follow the global trend and move toward a vision of the state more solidly grounded in democratic equality. In 1992, the Knesset (Israel's parliament) adopted a new Basic Law, which defines Israel's underlying political structure in lieu of a formal constitution. The legislation, called Basic Law: Human Dignity and Liberty, enumerated a series of individual rights intended to ensure that Israeli citizens were protected against government overreach. "The purpose of this Basic Law," the Knesset declared, "is to protect human dignity and liberty, in order to embed the values of the State of Israel as a Jewish and democratic state, in a Basic Law."

This Basic Law and another called Basic Law: Freedom of Occupation enacted around the same time transformed Israeli jurisprudence. Supreme Court justice Aharon Barak famously termed it a "constitutional revolution" in a 1992 speech—a view shared by many others in Israel at the time. For the first time, the Israeli state had provided its courts with clear tools to strike down Knesset legislation in the name of human rights. Moreover, the laws gave the Supreme Court authority to decide what it meant for Israel to be a Jewish *and* a democratic state.

Barak, who would later become the court's president, had a pretty clear idea of how to strike the balance. He believed "the State is Jewish, not in the religious sense, but in the sense that Jews have the right to immigrate here, and that their national experience is that of the State." Israel should use Hebrew as its official language, make Jewish holidays official holidays, and grant Jews abroad special rights to immigrate. But other than that, Barak argued, Israel's Jewish identity should be understood in terms of Jewish *values*—which are, more or less, liberal-democratic ones. "The fundamental values of Judaism—which we bequeathed to the whole world—are our basic values," he said. "I am referring to the values of love of humanity, sanctity of life, social justice, doing what is good and just, protecting human dignity, the rule of the law-maker, and other such eternal values."

There was thus, for Barak, no real conflict between Israel's Jewish identity and its democratic identity. In fact, he argued, the state's values could now be understood to include equality in a legal sense. Though the word "equality" did not literally appear in the text of any Basic Law, he found it to be implicit in the new Basic Laws' description of Israel as a democratic state. "The state is democratic, by recognizing institutions and organs built upon majority rule, by providing full equality among all its citizens and by its recognition of basic human and civil rights," he concluded.

In the coming years, Barak's vision would profoundly shape Israeli jurisprudence—perhaps most notably in ruling that the Basic Laws implicitly guaranteed equality among Israeli citizens. Although the court rarely overturned Knesset legislation, doing so only twenty-three times between 1992 and 2023, many of its rulings pushed Israel in a more egalitarian direction. One such decision held that residents of a mostly Arab town could not be taxed at a higher rate than their Jewish neighbors; another struck down a law exempting ultra-Orthodox men from national military service.

But there were limits to the Supreme Court's egalitarian efforts, chief among them its handling of the occupation, an issue on which the justices rarely intervened. And around the same time as the court worked to liberalize Israeli domestic law, the country's elected government attempted to resolve this even bigger threat to the state's democratic character. The Oslo Accords, a pair of agreements signed in 1993 and 1995, augured an end to the Israeli-Palestinian conflict. Israeli prime minister Yitzhak Rabin and Palestinian Liberation Organization chairman Yasser Arafat agreed to mutual recognition and a two-state solution to the conflict. The accords created the Palestinian Authority, an autonomous Palestinian political entity that would govern Gaza and the main population centers of the West Bank, as a kind of transitional step toward full independence.

Why did Rabin agree to a framework for voluntarily giving up Israeli-controlled land? In private, the prime minister expressed what his aide Jacques Neriah called "great and authentic anxiety" about the emergence of a "binational state" in Israel-Palestine. The flow of Jewish settlers into the West Bank and Gaza, tolerated and even encouraged by every Israeli government since 1967, was in his mind a form of slow-motion suicide—of Israel gradually destroying its Jewish and democratic character by forcing it to rule over a large and growing Palestinian noncitizen population. According to Neriah, Rabin believed that "his supreme task was to stop the policy of 'creeping annexation' of 'the territories.'"

The prime minister made a similar case to the Israeli public. In an October 1995 speech to the Knesset, Rabin argued that two things were needed to ensure a healthy future for Israel: to "first and foremost" retain a large Jewish majority, and at the same time to ensure that non-Jewish citizens enjoy "full personal, religious and civil rights, like those of any Israeli citizen [because] Judaism and racism are diametrically opposed." Any attempt to hold on to the Palestinian territories indefinitely would, in Rabin's telling, fatally undermine both those objectives. "Today, after innumerable wars and bloody incidents, we rule more than two million Palestinians through the IDF, and run their lives by a Civil Administration. This is not a peaceful solution," Rabin said. "We are convinced that a binational state with millions of Palestinian Arabs will not be able to fulfill the Jewish role of the State of Israel."

The centerpiece of Rabin's case for peace was thus the same concern for democratic equality that motivated Barak's constitutional revolution—but applied to an even more fundamental problem. In Rabin's mind, Israel simply could not survive as a democracy while ruling undemocratically over the Palestinian nation. Forced to choose between equality and hierarchy, Rabin opted for the former.

Put together, the constitutional revolution and the Oslo process amounted to a dire threat to the political status quo in Israel. The nation's model of ethnic democracy, which privileged Jews in all the lands it controlled, was being transformed from the inside. Israel's leaders were pioneering a very different vision for what the Israeli state could be, one that treated Israel's "Jewishness" as an organizing principle for the state's identity but not as a justification for excluding Arab citizens from politics or dominating Palestinians in the territories. If Barak and Rabin had had their way, Israel would have remained an ethnic democracy in only the loosest sense. Their visions sought to subordinate the principle of ethnicity to the democratic principle of equality.

"The confluence of liberalization and significant steps towards a peace process is not a coincidence," Israeli political scientist Dahlia Scheindlin wrote in her new book, *The Crooked Timber of Democracy in Israel*. "Control of the land and population of the Occupied Territories is inseparable from Israeli governance and society."

THE IDEOLOGY OF ISRAELI REACTION

The 1990s equality project took criticism from all sides: from the mainstream Jewish right for going too far, and from mainstream Palestinians and the Jewish left for not going far enough. But one line of attack that proved darkly influential came not from the mainstream but from the reactionary extreme. Its most influential advocate was a man named Meir Kahane.

An American-born rabbi, Kahane openly rejected both equality and democracy. He believed that Israel should be governed according to his hard-line interpretation of Jewish law, and that citizens had no right to contravene divine will at the ballot box. He held that Jews had a divine right to all the land of biblical Israel, which included the present-day West Bank and Gaza Strip. Palestinians had no place in Kahane's Greater Israel; he openly clamored for ethnic cleansing.

"The very majorityship of Jews will be threatened by the Arab birthrate. The result will be bloody conflict. If we hope to avoid this terrible result, there is only one path for us to take: the immediate transfer of Arabs from Eretz Yisrael, the Land of Israel, to their own lands," Kahane argued in his 1981 book, *They Must Go*, written while he was imprisoned by Israeli authorities on suspicion of planning terrorist attacks against Arabs.

Kahane embodied the reactionary spirit, objecting to Israeli democracy on grounds that it got in the way of enshrining Jewish dominance between the Jordan River and the Mediterranean Sea. "There is an ultimate insoluble contradiction between . . . the Jewish-Zionist state that was the millennial dream of the Jewish people and modern concepts of democracy and citizenship," Kahane wrote. His opponents "would allow Zionism and the Jewish state to be sacrificed on the altar of democracy."

By 1984, Kahane had attracted enough supporters that his Kach party managed to win a seat in the Knesset. He was treated with contempt by the mainstream: legislators on both the left and the right would walk out during his Knesset speeches. In 1988, Kach was banned from competing again in Israeli elections on grounds that it violated the country's laws against racist incitement. Two years later, Kahane was assassinated by a suspected al-Qaeda operative.

But Kahanism survived its namesake. As the country moved further and further toward democratic equality in the 1990s, his disciples turned to increasingly radical measures. In 1994, a West Bank settler and former Kach Knesset candidate named Baruch Goldstein opened fire on worshippers in the Muslim section of the Cave of the Patriarchs, a holy site for both Jews and Muslims near the West Bank city of Hebron. He killed twenty-nine people, including six under the age of fifteen. Goldstein's motives were plainly ideological: he had previously called for Arab expulsion and written that democracy was fundamentally incompatible with Jewish law. After the signing of the first Oslo Accord, he began wearing a yellow star with the German word *Jude* on it—implicitly equating Israel's leadership with Nazis.

Most Israelis reacted to Goldstein's acts with horror. Prime Minister Rabin declared in a Knesset speech that Goldstein "and those like him" were "a shame on Zionism and an embarrassment to Judaism." After the massacre, the Israeli government outlawed the Kach movement entirely.

Yigal Amir had a different reaction. A young anti-Arab extremist, he was further radicalized by Goldstein's atrocity and the public condemnation from the Israeli government—which he saw as a betrayal of the Jewish people. Goldstein's "spiritual readiness" to take matters into his own hands convinced Amir that he, too, needed to stop a looming disaster: the Oslo peace process. "It began after Goldstein. That's when I had the idea that it's necessary to take Rabin down," he said in one published interview.

In November 1995, moments after the prime minister had concluded a speech in Tel Aviv calling for peace, Amir took out a pistol and fired two shots into his back. Before the night was over, Yitzhak Rabin had died.

At the time, it seemed like those two terrorist attacks may have been the last gasp of an Israeli reactionary spirit in terminal decline. The headwinds were blowing in equality's favor; the reactionaries appeared electorally impotent, reduced to acts of terrorism rather than seriously contesting elections. But that's not what happened.

In 1995, weeks before Rabin's assassination, a nineteen-year-old named Itamar Ben-Gvir charged the prime minister's automobile. "We got to his car, and we'll get to him too," Ben-Gvir said in a televised interview while holding a hood ornament that he had ripped off of Rabin's Cadillac. As I write, Ben-Gvir—who had a portrait of Goldstein in his living room and supports a pardon for Amir—is serving in the Israeli cabinet as minister of national security.

He's in charge of the Israeli police.

THE RISE OF BENJAMIN NETANYAHU— AND THE DECLINE OF ISRAELI DEMOCRACY

As is typical in an advanced democracy, the reactionary spirit's more overt manifestations—Kahane's outright calls to dismantle democracy, Goldstein's and Amir's violence—repulsed the Israeli mainstream. The dominant parties in their wake remained Rabin's center-left Labor, champion of secularism and the peace process, and Benjamin Netanyahu's Likud, at the time a center-right party that opposed the peace process but did not manage to derail it during Netanyahu's late-nineties stint in power. Over the next decade, Israel experienced a series of traumas that fundamentally discredited the center left in the eyes of much of the public—and set the stage for a lurch in Kahane's direction.

The reactionary surge began with the failure of the peace process. Rabin's Labor Party successor, Ehud Barak, was unable to come to terms with Yasser Arafat in a series of negotiations in 1999 and 2000. That failure led to the violence of the Second Intifada, a bloody conflict that stretched between 2000 and 2005, characterized by intense ground combat in the occupied territories and suicide bombings on Israeli civilian targets in cities like Tel Aviv. Shortly after the end of the Second Intifada, Israel tried a different tack: unilateral withdrawal of troops and settlers from the Gaza Strip. The process, initiated by a center-right government, was supposed to free Israel from any security responsibilities in Gaza. But less than two years later, Hamas launched a rebellion against the Palestinian Authority and seized control over the Gaza Strip. This set the stage for nearly two more decades of conflict: a punishing Israeli blockade, periodic rocket fire out of Gaza, and semiregular escalation to full-scale war between the two sides.

The Palestinians, as the weaker side, always bore the brunt of the casualties in this fighting. But Israelis suffered too. Hamas's suicide bombings during the Second Intifada and rocket volleys out of Gaza soured the country on the left's vision of Israelis and Palestinians living side by side in peace. Many Israelis concluded that, after the rejection of Oslo and subsequent violence, there was "no partner for peace" on the Palestinian side—and that the right's critique of the peace process had got something right. One study, by political scientists Anna Getmansky and Thomas Zeitzoff, found that rocket fire increased support for right-wing parties by two to six points in areas within the projectiles' range. The

Labor Party, which had dominated Israeli politics for several decades, lost election after election—and now struggles to win enough votes to make it into the Knesset at all. Meretz, the long-standing left-wing party, fell out of the Knesset entirely in the 2022 elections.

Initially, the decline of the left primarily benefited the center right. Between 2001 and 2009, every prime minister hailed from Likud or Kadima, a Likud breakaway faction that drew from the party's more centrist wing. Israeli voters during this decade were not rejecting the left for ideological reasons per se; contemporary polls still showed majority support for a two-state solution in theory. Rather, the public believed that peace was at present *unrealistic*—a point often made by the right—and adjusted their voting behavior as such. The mainstream politics of the 2000s were not those of the reactionary spirit; they were right leaning but still committed to maintaining some kind of balance between the Israeli principles of ethnicity and equality.

Yet at the same time, a significant percentage of the Israeli population was moving in a reactionary direction. A pair of right-wing parties epitomized the far right's rising electoral fortunes: Yisrael Beiteinu, a secular nationalist party primarily supported by Russian immigrants, and Jewish Home, a settler party that outflanked both Likud and Yisrael Beiteinu from the hard right. Founded in 2008, Jewish Home's central cause was permanent expansion of settlement outposts and ultimate annexation of the majority of the West Bank. Palestinians, under this arrangement, would be denied either a state or Israeli citizenship—disenfranchised in a manner similar to the marginalization of Blacks in the Jim Crow South. Partly by consolidating far-right tendencies that had existed since the country's early history in parties like the National Religious

Party, the Jewish Home became a reactionary force to be reckoned with.

One man above all others was responsible for bringing this style of extreme politics into the Israeli mainstream: Likud leader Benjamin Netanyahu. During his historically long stretch in power, from 2009 to 2021, Netanyahu pushed Israel far to the reactionary right—and nearly singlehandedly caused a democratic crisis.

Netanyahu, frequently referred to by his nickname Bibi, resembles his longtime acquaintance Viktor Orbán in a number of important respects. Like Orbán, he has a background that resonates with his citizens; his brother Yonatan was a national hero who died rescuing Jewish hostages in Uganda in 1976. Like Orbán, Netanyahu did not rule as a reactionary extremist during his first government (1996–1999). And also like Orbán, Netanyahu did not fully accept that his first defeat was legitimate. He blamed his loss in the 1999 elections on a hostile press corps, grousing to a wealthy ally that "I need my own media" to win future elections. In 2007, a billionaire American Jewish supporter of Netanyahu named Sheldon Adelson founded a newspaper, *Israel Hayom*, that basically served as a pro-Netanyahu propaganda sheet. Distributed for free on Israel's streets, the paper rapidly became the most-read print outlet in the country.

Adelson's investment certainly helped Netanyahu win the 2009 election. But even with such generous support, his Likud did not marshal anything like Fidesz's two-thirds majority in the Hungarian parliament. Israel's proportional representation system allows parties to win Knesset seats with very small percentages of the national vote, making it nearly impossible for a single party to win an outright majority (let alone a supermajority). In 2009, Likud actually placed second in total seats;

it only got to govern because the first-place party, Kadima, couldn't negotiate a coalition agreement with enough smaller parties to form a governing majority.

But despite his relative weakness, Netanyahu still started down the Orbánist path—most infamously with the media. As prime minister, Netanyahu reportedly held a series of private meetings with Israeli media executives to talk about tilting coverage in his direction. There is significant evidence that he succeeded with Walla, a major online news portal, striking a deal to approve a merger with Walla's parent company in exchange for pro-Bibi reporting. In 2015, Walla reporter Amir Tibon wrote some measured criticism of Netanyahu's handling of security issues—only for an editor to kill the article. "We can't publish this. You know what the circumstances are right now," Tibon recalled the editor saying.

At the same time, Netanyahu publicly aligned himself with the far right. He brought Yisrael Beiteinu into his governing coalition in 2009, followed by the Jewish Home party after it quadrupled its vote in the 2013 election. Instead of domesticating its radicals, Netanyahu came to embrace their causes. During the 2015 elections, he fully repudiated the two-state solution, saying, "If I'm elected there won't be a Palestinian state," and warned his supporters to turn out to the polls because "Arab voters are coming out in droves." The implication—that Arab participation in Israeli politics is necessarily illegitimate—was lost on no one.

His reactionary rhetoric was matched by reactionary policy. According to research by Adalah, a Palestinian-run human rights organization in Israel, the country enacted roughly sixty-two laws discriminating against Arab citizens between 1948 and 2017. Nearly half of them were passed between 2009 and 2017, including laws suspending certain due process rights for people detained on "security" charges (disproportionately Arabs), and another legalizing the use of American-style "stop and frisk" policing techniques (which can encourage racial profiling).

In 2018, Netanyahu's government passed something even bigger: a new Basic Law that implicitly redefined Arabs as second-class citizens. The text of the law officially recognizes Israel as "the nation state of the Jewish people," holding that "the exercise of the right to national self-determination in the State of Israel is unique to the Jewish People." On the surface, this may seem like nothing more than the codification of the basic Zionist idea of Israel as a Jewish state. In actuality, the law was worded to ensure that non-Jews could not have equal standing. The Knesset has "passed a law of Jewish supremacy and told us that we will always be second-class citizens," Ayman Odeh, an Arab member of Knesset (MK) from the Joint List party, said in a statement after the law's passage.

Ayelet Shaked, a Jewish Home MK who was Netanyahu's justice minister at the time, said something similar in a 2018 speech (albeit in veiled language). Arguing that "the state should say that there is a place to maintain the Jewish majority even if it violates rights," she claimed that the bill would provide a Jewish counterweight to the Supreme Court's allegedly excessive concern for democracy and equality. "From a constitutional point of view there is an advantage to democracy, [but] it must be balanced. And the Supreme Court should be given another constitutional tool that will also give power to Judaism," Shaked said. "There are places where the character of the State of Israel as a Jewish state must be maintained—and this sometimes comes at the expense of equality."

Reining in the judiciary, which had thrown up occa-sional limited roadblocks to the settlement enterprise, was a special aim of Netanyahu's various governments. During Shaked's 2015–2019 tenure as justice minister, the government made a variety of moves to impose political control on the courts—including, for example, stripping the Supreme Court of jurisdiction over certain West Bank land issues and hand-ing it over to a friendlier lower court. By the end of her time in office, Shaked was openly bragging that she had "broken" the Barak-era conception of the court as guarantor of equality.

And if attacks on the media, ethnic minorities, and the independent judiciary weren't enough to suggest paral-lels to Orbán, Netanyahu also went after civil society and dissidents—with a special focus on anti-occupation leftists. In 2018, Israel passed a law prohibiting particular groups that allegedly impugned the IDF and the state's legitimacy from entering schools or talking to students. The law was dubbed the "Breaking the Silence" law as it was all but explicitly tar-geted at repressing Yehuda Shaul's organization. The govern-ment also passed laws enabling civil suits against people who advocated boycotting Israeli goods, and outright banning foreign boycott advocates from entering the country. In 2019, the latter was used to deport Israeli resident Omar Shakir, the American director of Israel-Palestine issues for Human Rights Watch.

But like successful reactionaries around the world, and unlike Kahane, Netanyahu and his allies did not openly reject basic democratic principles. The attack on the courts, for example, was not billed as an effort to remove constraints on settlement growth and Netanyahu's power but rather as an effort to retake democratic control from unelected judges. The coalition's leaders treated allegations of authoritarianism as offensive, even absurd. Shaked once released a campaign ad where she sprays herself with a perfume bottle labeled "fascism" and says to the camera that the fragrance "smells like democracy to me."

This campaign to destroy democracy in the name of saving it began escalating further in 2019, the year Netanyahu was formally indicted on criminal charges. The charges were, broadly speaking, related to allegations of corruption—the most serious of which stemmed from his reported crooked deal with Walla. Rather than resigning and fighting the charges as a private citizen, Netanyahu declared war on the Israeli justice system, labeling the entire case a conspiracy against him by the courts and an alleged Israeli "deep state." Even Israel's attorney general, a longtime Netanyahu ally, was supposedly in on it. The prime minister and his party escalated their war on the courts, floating legislation that would allow the Knesset to override court rulings and immunize incumbent prime ministers from prosecution.

This behavior revealed Netanyahu to be exactly the sort of person the indictment alleged he was: one willing to attack the very foundations of Israeli democracy to secure his hold on power. Netanyahu's right-wing politics and self-interest had led him to embrace a fully reactionary package, including the aggressively antidemocratic strategy for fighting his indictment. His new stance proved too much for even the leadership of Yisrael Beiteinu and the Jewish Home. These parties, once the far-right fringe of Israeli politics, would soon join with the center and the left to oppose Netanyahu's assault on democracy.

Between 2019 and 2021, the question of Netanyahu's fitness for office paralyzed Israeli politics; the electorate polarized into pro-Netanyahu and anti-Netanyahu camps. With neither side able to command a durable majority, the country held four successive elections in two years. Finally, in 2021, the opposition struck an unlikely agreement: a broad coalition of parties from across the political spectrum, including (for the first time in history) an Arab party, formed a slim governing majority united solely by opposition to Netanyahu.

But this left-to-right coalition could not last long and fell apart after about a year under the weight of its own contradictions. In the November 2022 elections, a new faction rose to replace Jewish Home as the standard-bearer for the reactionary right: Religious Zionism, an extreme-right alliance that included Itamar Ben-Gvir's Kahanist Jewish Power party. Religious Zionism won nearly 11 percent of the national vote, good for the third-most seats in the Knesset. During the campaign, Ben-Gvir was, along with faction leader Bezalel Smotrich, Religious Zionism's public face.

During his rise, Ben-Gvir nominally rejected Kahane's most extreme antidemocratic positions. Speaking at an annual Kahane memorial in 2022—an event he attended every year—he drew boos from the crowd for saying "it's no secret that today I am not Rabbi Kahane, and don't support expulsion of all the Arabs" (merely the ones he deemed "terrorists," he later clarified). In a December 2022 speech after his victory, Ben-Gvir accused the center-left opposition parties of being "backwards, illiberal people who are unable to accept different opinions, and you are not aligned with the democratic regime."

But few doubted the sincerity of his Kahanist convictions; again, he had literally hung a portrait of Baruch Goldstein in his living room. Ben-Gvir maintained a democratic veneer by describing "democracy" as pure majority rule, arguing that his support for undermining judicial independence was actually a quest to protect democracy against unelected judges. It was the classic liberalism-versus-democracy move long beloved by reactionaries, one used effectively by Netanyahu and others on the Israeli right. In Israel, it's a powerful enough line that even a cartoonish reactionary like Ben-Gvir could use it to purchase some kind of nominal democratic credentials.

The fact that this truly extreme brand of far-right politics could thrive in contemporary Israel showed just how deeply the reactionary spirit had seeped into parts of the Israeli polity. The Israeli Democracy Index, an annual nonpartisan survey, found that the percentage of Jewish Israelis who believed "Jewish citizens of Israel should have more rights than non-Jewish citizens" climbed from 27 percent in 2018 to 49 percent in 2022.

Netanyahu's 2022 coalition also relied on two ultra-Orthodox parties that had themselves drifted in an increasingly reactionary direction. This wasn't a result of the Palestinian conflict. Historically, these parties had been neutral or even potentially supportive of a two-state agreement. Rather, it was in response to the other great component of the 1990s push for equality: the constitutional revolution championed by Barak and others. Ultra-Orthodox parties aimed to secure special privileges for their community (like exemptions from mandatory military service) and expand religion's role in public life (by, for example, maintaining a ban on same-sex marriage and keeping public transit closed on Shabbat). The modern court's rulings pushing Israel toward social equality—most notably in ruling against ultra-Orthodox conscription exemptions—radicalized these parties against the legal system. They became willing partners in Netanyahu's and the far-right's war on the judiciary.

The post-2022 coalition was really about the convergence of three different kinds of reactionaries. The far right wanted de facto annexation of the West Bank and further restrictions on Arab rights inside Israel proper. The ultra-Orthodox wanted to codify an unequal idea of citizenship privileging their community while expanding religion's role in public life. And Netanyahu wanted to stay out of jail and in power indefinitely. Each of these goals could be accomplished, in their minds, by seizing political control over the courts. This is why the coalition's first act in 2023 was to propose a total overhaul of the balance of power between Israel's judiciary and the Knesset. The bill contained a laundry list of proposals aimed at putting the court under the prime minister's thumb. Some of the most egregious were giving the legislature power to override any court ruling with a simple majority vote, and placing the Knesset majority fully in charge of appointing judges (the current system gives primary authority to a panel that includes a mix of elected politicians, judges, and legal professionals).

Now, weakening the judiciary can be a perfectly legitimate—maybe even valuable—policy goal for legislators to pursue. But its wisdom depends on the institutional setup of the country in question: Does the country suffer from too many checks and balances, making it hard to change the laws, or is it more at risk from a dangerous concentration of power in elected officials' hands? The specific design of the overhaul and the objectives of the political forces pushing the courts also matter. Are the elected officials' proposals actually helping fix a real problem, or are they instead a veiled authoritarian power grab?

The Israeli overhaul proposals flunk nearly all of these tests. In Israel, the judiciary is the *only* real check on the government. If Netanyahu's legislation were to pass, the prime minister's office would become a kind of elected dictatorship: a position whose power was formally constrained by elections alone. Given Netanyahu's autocratic track record, the dangerous ambitions of his coalition partners, and the sheer degree of power they would acquire if the overhaul proposal were to pass, the legislation appeared to be a recipe for democratic disaster.

Specifically, the judicial overhaul would permit the Knesset to shield Netanyahu from prosecution and to launch more power grabs. It would pave the way for Smotrich and Ben-Gvir to deepen the occupation and further marginalize Arab citizens as they pleased. It would ensure that the Orthodox maintain their privileged position in the country's religious hierarchy, expanding their ability to reduce legal protections for secular and more liberal religious Jews.

In effect, the resulting Israeli political system would be one where Netanyahu and his allies governed without constraint—allowing the Hungarianization of Israel to continue apace.

AGAINST ILLIBERAL DEMOCRACY—
FOR ISRAEL AND THE WORLD

Israeli democracy was not going down without a fight. The judicial overhaul prompted the largest street demonstrations in Israeli history, months of chaos and mass demonstrations that forced Netanyahu to temporarily shelve the legislation in March. (We'll have a more detailed discussion of the protest movement, and the general lessons it contains for fighting the reactionary spirit, in Chapter 7.)

But with the judicial overhaul being the government's raison d'être, they refused to give up in the face of public pressure. So in the summer, they tried a different tack: passing the bill in piecemeal form, one provision at a time. In July, the government muscled through a partial ban on the so-called reasonableness doctrine, a legal tool used by courts to overturn cabinet decisions, as an amendment to the Basic Law on the judiciary. The protests escalated, Netanyahu's poll numbers dropped, and the country geared up for another round of deeply divisive battle over the next bill in the court overhaul package.

Before the prime minister could pass it, disaster struck. On October 7, Hamas operatives broke through inadequately defended outposts on the Gaza border, killing over 1,200 and taking over 240 captive. More Israelis died that day than during the entire Second Intifada. It was the single greatest loss of life not only in Israeli history but in all of Jewish history since the Holocaust.

Israel's response was swift and brutal. The Israel Defense Forces killed thousands of Palestinians via aerial bombardment and caused a humanitarian crisis by cutting off water, electricity, and fuel supplies to the Gaza Strip. A subsequent ground invasion of the Strip, paired with continued intense bombing, did real damage to Hamas but also significantly increased the death toll. In just the first hundred days of fighting, upwards of twenty thousand Palestinians had been killed, and roughly 85 percent of the Strip's population had been displaced.

The tension between the country's reactionary and democratic identities has been on display throughout Israel's reaction to the October 7 attack. On the reactionary side, both Ben Gvir and Smotrich called for ethnically cleansing the Gaza Strip and reestablishing settlements there. Other extreme members of the Knesset employed outright genocidal language; Religious Zionism MK Amihai Eliyahu, for example, signaled that Israel might consider nuking Gaza. Even some relatively centrist figures, like President Isaac Herzog, suggested that Palestinian civilians might be legitimate military targets. With Israeli authorities' attention diverted, settlers intensified attacks on Palestinians in the West Bank. Some domestic critics of the war effort were harassed by the police and even arrested.

On the democratic side, Israel's institutions have continued operating despite wartime pressures. Perhaps most notably, the Supreme Court issued a landmark ruling overturning the reasonableness ban—the first time it had ever overturned any part of a Basic Law. Moreover, the Israeli public has also refused to let Netanyahu off the hook—with many blaming Israel's tragedy on his government's reactionary agenda. Some argued that Netanyahu's preoccupation with the courts created an internal crisis that Hamas sought to exploit. Others argued that the far right's obsession with colonizing the West Bank had diverted Israeli troops from where they were most needed. At least some of these arguments resonated: every survey taken in the months after the war began showed Likud's numbers cratering, suggesting the party would lose roughly 40 percent of its seats in elections. These developments—the court ruling and the collapse in Netanyahu's support—led many Israeli commentators to declare the entire judicial overhaul finished, a political impossibility in Israel's new post–October 7 political reality.

These wartime developments, and the months of protest that preceded them, underscore that the country's "house divided" problem is still intensifying. It's a situation that tells us something important about the sources of the reactionary spirit's power, both in Israel and around the world: that formally incorporating illiberal principles into a democracy does not domesticate the reactionary spirit. Rather, it fans reaction's flames.

The reactionary spirit is an almost inevitable feature of democratic life anywhere. Democracy encourages political challenges to existing hierarchies; that some defenders of hierarchy will turn against democracy in response is guaranteed. But the reactionary spirit is not equally strong in every country and at every time. Contemporary Israel illustrates one way in which it can grow especially powerful: when one of the central hierarchies in question, in this case the privileged status of Jews over Arabs, is formally incorporated into law.

The occupation's defenders believe that Israel is entitled to rule over Palestinians indefinitely while denying them citizenship or any social rights. It's hardly a far leap from this conviction to supporting both extreme violence against Palestinians and attacks on rights for other Israelis. The belief structure already depends on the idea that some people count and others don't. If the Schmittian enemy includes Palestinians in the West Bank and Gaza, then why not Palestinian citizens of Israel? And if Arab citizens can be enemies, then why not Jews who ally with them to protest the occupation?

These are not abstract questions. The occupation is not just a construct, but rather a very concrete set of bureaucratic and military policies laid out in Israeli law. Enforcing Jewish supremacy in the occupied territories introduces authoritarian rules and ideas into the Israeli political system, legitimizing them in the eyes of the broader public. Much as the existence of slave states side by side with free ones gave rise to the Fugitive Slave Act and criminalization of abolitionist speech, the existence of Israeli democracy side by side with West Bank military rule necessitates some kind of bleed-over from the authoritarian side to the democratic one.

This authoritarian creep was not made inevitable by Israel defining itself as a Jewish state. Many countries have some official religious or ethnic identity without endangering democracy. King Charles is still the formal head of the Church of England; ethnic Germans have long been given preferential immigration rights by Berlin. Aharon Barak envisioned Israel becoming something like those leading European states. But so long as the occupation exists, proponents of a far-right vision of the Jewish-democratic balance have natural allies in its defenders (the two groups have significant overlap). Their shared idea is that Israel is a state for Jews in a very exclusive sense—a vision that justifies the creation of tiers of rights and citizenship for people based on their identity. For this reason, the great battles over peace and the judiciary cannot truly be separated from each other.

And make no mistake: this shared struggle will tilt increasingly in favor of reactionary forces as long as the occupation remains in place. For Jewish Israelis, extending citizenship to Palestinians in Gaza and the West Bank is an impossibility. It would make Arabs a majority, functionally ending Israel's status as a Jewish state and thus (in their eyes) its central reason to exist. And if democracy cannot move eastward, then perpetual occupation means authoritarianism creeping westward, the Israeli democratic system accommodating itself more and more to the governing logic of the occupation. The fight over the Supreme Court was, for Israel's prodemocracy forces, a defensive action. Going on offense requires a push for peace—a goal that feels far away indeed, even more so after Hamas's horrific attack and Israel's subsequent brutalization of Gaza.

As unique as the Israeli predicament seems, it offers an important general lesson: that the reactionary spirit is not satisfied with half measures. It is very difficult to strike a durable balance between formalized inequality and democracy; eventually, one component of a society's identity will come to dominate the other. This is the essential flaw at the heart of the notion of illiberal democracy, a broad type of democracy that's a kind of political cousin to Smooha's idea of ethnic democracy.

The term "illiberal democracy," coined by scholar and CNN host Fareed Zakaria in a 1997 *Foreign Affairs* article, refers to a government type that mixes free elections with an untrammeled executive and restrictions on individual or minority rights. Elections may be both free and fair, but the governments they authorize face very few constraints on their powers. In our current reactionary moment, illiberal democracy has become a popular cause for those looking to confer democratic legitimacy on undeniably antiliberal projects—a group ranging from leaders like Viktor Orbán to influential "postliberal" intellectuals in the West.

"The new state that we are building is an illiberal state," Orbán declared in a 2014 speech, insisting that "[while] not liberal, it still can be a democracy." Hungary's new model, he said in another speech four years later, centered partly on the "illiberal concept" of giving "priority to Christian culture" in its policies.

We can say confidently, in Orbán's case, that the theory is cover for his autocratic project. But such ideas are being taken seriously by politicians and activists and intellectuals—which makes it important to highlight the ways Israel's experience directly challenges their theory. When Israel's ethnic identity strayed into illiberal territory, becoming a justification for the exclusion of Arab Palestinians and Jewish dissenters from the polity, it created profound tension with the state's democratic character. Because democracy depends on an ideal of equality, illiberal politics premised on equality's rejection have a tendency to turn on democracy itself. So-called illiberal democracy is often just Schmittian authoritarianism by another name.

Israel's recent history should also be a cautionary tale for mainstream political forces in healthier democracies, who have at times followed Netanyahu's approach of accommodating themselves to reactionary politics. Tarik Abou-Chadi, a political scientist at Oxford, has extensively studied the consequences of European center-left and center-right parties' attempts to weaken the far right by moving in its direction on immigration and identity issues. He found that it didn't work. If anything, mainstream parties that compromised improved extremists' performance in elections. "When mainstream parties pick up radical right issues, they rather run the risk of legitimizing and normalizing radical right discourse and strengthening the radical right in the long run," he wrote in a 2022 paper (coauthored by Werner Krause and Denis Cohen).

The more a country incorporates an illiberal contempt for equality into its law and politics, the weaker its democratic foundations will become. We saw this first in the American experience with slavery and Jim Crow, and we are seeing it today in Israel's experience with the occupation. The rest of the world should take notice.

CHAPTER 6

INDIA, AMERICA, AND CHINA

On June 22, 2023, I was standing in the rain on the White House South Lawn, waiting for President Joe Biden to receive one of democracy's greatest enemies.

Indian prime minister Narendra Modi, the chief executive of what he terms "the Mother of Democracy," had long been a true believer in a radical Hindu-nationalist ideology called Hindutva—a movement founded on the rejection of India's core constitutional commitment to being a secular country of all its citizens. To better implement the Hindutva agenda, Modi took a hammer to the foundations of Indian democracy, weakening core checks on his own power like the rule of law and the free press. Less than three months prior to Modi's visit to Washington, an Indian court had sentenced opposition leader Rahul Gandhi to prison for two years for a campaign-trail joke about the prime minister's last name—a comment, the court ruled, that defamed "the entire Modi community."

The prime minister's party, the BJP, used the ruling as an excuse to kick Gandhi out of parliament.

Yet Modi was being greeted at the White House with a rare honor. At that point, the Biden administration had only hosted official state dinners for two other leaders: the presidents of South Korea and France, both democratic treaty allies. India was not such an ally and, under Modi, barely still qualified as a democracy. But nonetheless, America was pulling out all the stops. The streets of Washington were decked out in Indian flags; a crowd of thousands, primarily Indians and Indian Americans, had assembled outside the White House to cheer the prime minister's arrival.

The real reason for the pomp and circumstance was obvious: Biden wanted to court India as an ally against a rising China. Modi's nation isn't just the world's largest democracy by population; it's the largest country period, having passed China sometime in spring 2023. It's a nuclear-armed power and one of the fastest-growing economies, likely to become the world's third-largest economy by 2030. It shares a long and tense land border with China; in 2020 and 2021, the two countries fought a series of skirmishes in which dozens of soldiers were killed. It makes perfect geopolitical sense that the US should want to try to draw India closer into its embrace.

But as much strategic sense as the visit made, it was a clear moral embarrassment for America. The US president found himself praising India's democracy under Modi at a joint press conference, skipping over the irony that Modi hadn't held a single solo presser during his entire nine years in office. Only two reporters were allowed to ask questions; one of the questions, from a Muslim American reporter at the *Wall Street Journal* named Sabrina Siddiqui, focused on Modi's human rights and democracy record. The prime minister's angry response—in the room, you could feel his affront at the challenge—was nothing but bluster. And in the days that followed, Siddiqui, who is herself South Asian, came under vicious attack from Modi's fans in India and even some BJP politicians. The reaction was so cruel, so dangerous, that the White House was forced to intervene on her behalf.

"Democracy," in short, was never truly on display during Modi's official reception; it was raw power politics all the way down. This was an even deeper betrayal of American ideals than it seems: Narendra Modi is, for all his democratic rhetoric, actually a greater threat to the future of global democracy than Xi Jinping, the president of China. It is very hard to weaken democracy from the outside in countries where it is already established. For China to wield this level of influence, Beijing would need to either pass Washington as the world's most powerful government or build a political model that inspired copycat movements around the world. So far, there is no reason to believe either of those things have happened or will happen in the near future.

But India under Modi poses a more insidious danger. Hindutva is a long-standing and powerful expression of the Indian reactionary spirit, one that currently seeks to redefine "democracy" to mean its opposite. If Modi succeeds in transforming Indian secular democracy into a Hindu-nationalist version of Orbán's Hungary, he will send a powerful signal that his kind of competitive authoritarianism is a viable political model going forward—especially if the United States continues moving in the same direction. If India fully succumbs, a strategic alignment between it and the US will be a striking example of hypocrisy on America's part, the kind of hit to its moral credibility that in the past has severely limited its ability to win supporters for its stated vision of a free future.

The survival of democracy in the twenty-first century depends less on the struggle between the United States and China and more about conflicts *inside* America and India. And in India, democracy's champions are on the brink of defeat.

THE RISE OF REACTIONARY INDIA

In 1939, while India was under British rule, a prominent Indian activist named M. S. Golwalkar published a book titled *We, or Our Nationhood Defined*. The book codified the ideology of Golwalkar's popular organization, a Hindu-nationalist movement called the Rashtriya Swayamsevak Sangh (RSS). One contemporary observer, an American political scientist named Jean Curran, referred to the book as the RSS "Bible."

The RSS nominally supported independence, though it did comparatively little to advance the cause. Its sectarian vision for India after independence was very different from the mainstream anticolonial movement embodied by Mahatma Gandhi, Jawaharlal Nehru, and their Indian National Congress party (known informally as Congress). In *We*, Golwalkar argued that all nations are defined by five traits: shared land, shared race, shared religion, shared culture, and shared language. Based on this definition, the entirety of what he called Hindusthan—comprising modern India, Pakistan, and Bangladesh—rightfully belonged to the Hindu nation and the Hindu nation alone. The many millions of Muslims residing in the territory were not potential citizens in a future Indian state, but rather enemies, people who "take themselves to be the conquering invaders and grasp for power." Gandhi's belief of an Indian nation "composed of all those who happened to reside therein" was a delusion, one fueled by "wrong notions of democracy."

So what was to be done with Muslims and other minorities in a Hindu state? Golwalkar's solution was simple: they either become Hindus or be stripped of legal rights. "The foreign races in Hindusthan must either adopt the Hindu culture and language, must learn to respect and hold in reverence Hindu religion, must entertain no idea but those of the glorification of the Hindu race and culture, i.e., of the Hindu nation and must lose their separate existence to merge in the Hindu race, or may stay in the country, wholly subordinated to the Hindu nation, claiming nothing, deserving no privileges, far less any preferential treatment—not even citizen's rights," he wrote. "There is [or] at least should be no other course for them to adopt. We are an old nation; let us deal, as old nations ought to and do deal, with the foreign races, who have chosen to live in our country."

Stunningly, at least to contemporary ears, Golwalkar cited Nazi mistreatment of German Jews as a *positive* example for Hindusthan. "To keep up the purity of the Race and its culture, Germany shocked the world by her purging the country of the Semitic Races—the Jews. Race pride at its highest has been manifested here," Golwalkar wrote. "Germany has also shown how well-nigh impossible it is for Races and cultures, having differences going to the root, to be assimilated into one united whole, a good lesson for us in Hindusthan to learn and profit by."

This was not mere rhetoric. In the 1920s and 1930s, the RSS sent representatives to Italy and Germany to learn from fascist governments there. Christophe Jaffrelot, a leading French specialist on Indian politics, refers to the RSS's ideology, Hindutva, as an "Indian version of fascism"; its early doctrine was directly and self-consciously modeled after fascist ideas and practices.

Golwalkar's book crystallized the Indian reactionary spirit. Read in its entirety, *We* is a blistering response to Gandhi and the mainstream Indian national movement, a polemic arguing that their vision of democratic equality was a betrayal of the true nation. In Golwalkar's potted history, Hindus have always been the (rightfully) dominant power in Hindusthan. Gandhi and the Congress posed a threat to the restoration of the Hindu nation, making them no less an enemy of Hindus than the British colonial overlords. In fact, he argued, Congress and the British were in cahoots, their vision of "equality" working to sap the Hindu nation of the vitality it needed to throw off colonial rule. "This new force—the British—is well aware of the strength of Hindusthan, and knows that it lies in the Hindu National consciousness. Systematic attempts were, therefore, made to weed it out," he wrote. "The crown of such and many other denationalizing activities was the foundation of the so-called 'Indian National Congress.' . . . The express aim of founding this body was to suppress all National outbursts, likely to dethrone the British power."

In January 1948, about nine years after *We*'s publication and just five months after India finally attained independence, Mahatma Gandhi was assassinated by a fanatical RSS member named Nathuram Godse. Godse had attempted to kill Gandhi twice before; Gandhi, as was his practice, refused to press charges under British colonial law. Godse's third assassination attempt, according to his own statements, was motivated by partition, the split between India and Pakistan following independence. Partition was almost unimaginably bloody, with partisans on both sides committing atrocities that produced refugee crises on both sides of the border. This calamity, and the loss of land that RSS partisans saw as rightfully part of Hindusthan, was too much for Godse to bear.

"When top leaders of Congress, with the consent of Gandhi, divided and tore the country—which we consider a deity of worship—my mind was filled with direful anger," Godse said in a court statement.

Godse's account is full of falsehoods. For one, Gandhi actually opposed partition partly on grounds that Hindus and Muslims alike could live under a shared and equal state. But Godse was gripped by the idea that any effort at equality (in this case, two democratic states for two religious groups) was an intolerable assault on the rightful order of things. Like Yigal Amir decades later, he saw little hope in the political system and decided instead to take matters into his own violent hands.

There are striking similarities between the Israeli and Indian reactionary spirits. In both countries, the reactionary spirit derives its force from a foundational division between the dominant ethnocultural group (Jews and Hindus) and Muslims. In both cases, politics for several decades after independence was dominated by center-left factions (Labor in Israel, Congress in India) which rendered reactionary factions relatively marginal. And in both cases, those dominant parties faltered in the face of a modern surge in reactionary sentiment sparked by intensifying political struggle over equality.

But unlike Israel, India began as a secular state clearly dedicated to the equality of all its citizens, with its constitution explicitly prohibiting discrimination "on grounds only of religion, race, caste, sex, place of birth or any of them" from the outset. Across India, citizens speak dozens of languages and hail from hundreds of different ethnic groups. A number of different religions flourish—not just Hinduism and Islam but also Sikhism, Jainism, Christianity, and Buddhism. India's caste system, derived from Hindu scripture but applied more generally, divides the population into thousands of different groups based on birth and lineage. Members of upper castes, like Brahmins, not only tend to be wealthier but also enjoy significant social privileges relative to their lower-caste peers. Members of the lowest castes, the Dalits or Scheduled Castes, have long been subject to a kind of discrimination called untouchability: the higher castes refuse to eat with them and demand that their children be segregated in schools.

India's founders did not believe such a complex and divided society could survive as an ethnoreligious state of the sort envisioned by Golwalkar. Nehru, India's first prime minister, thought that such a system would "not only [be] wrong in itself but will inevitably lead to friction and trouble." He insisted on a secular state, one where Muslims and other religious minorities were not only tolerated but provided the same rights as any other Indian citizen.

B. R. Ambedkar, the chair of the committee that drafted India's constitution, took this logic even further. Ambedkar was a brilliant lawyer and a Dalit activist who had spent decades campaigning against the caste system (an inequality on which the Brahmin Nehru was relatively silent). In November 1949, just two months before the constitution would go into effect, Ambedkar gave a speech in parliament arguing that Indian democracy depended not only on legal equality but also on a deeper movement to level social hierarchies. For if democracy promised equality but failed to deliver it, those at the bottom would revolt:

> On the 26th of January 1950, we are going to enter into a life of contradictions. In politics we will have equality and in social and economic life we will have inequality. In politics we will be recognizing the principle of one man one vote and one vote one value. In our social and economic life,

we shall, by reason of our social and economic structure, continue to deny the principle of one man one value. How long shall we continue to live this life of contradictions? How long shall we continue to deny equality in our social and economic life? If we continue to deny it for long, we will do so only by putting our political democracy in peril. We must remove this contradiction at the earliest possible moment or else those who suffer from inequality will blow up the structure of political democracy which this Assembly has so laboriously built up.

Early India took Nehru's and Ambedkar's concerns seriously. The new state prohibited religious discrimination, religious curricula in public schools, and any use of tax money for promoting religion. It outlawed untouchability and introduced the world's very first affirmative action system for Dalits and certain marginalized tribal groups. India's founders did not, like their peers in Israel or the early United States, build an identity crisis into their new state. There was no question as to where India's government was supposed to stand in the grand conflict between hierarchy and equality.

For roughly thirty years after independence, India appeared relatively committed to its egalitarian promise. The RSS's first political wing, called the Bharatiya Jana Sangh (BJS), failed to ever reach double digits in a national election. During this period, it was not the far right that posed the greatest threat to Indian democracy but rather Congress itself. Between 1975 and 1977, Prime Minister Indira Gandhi suspended civil rights and ruled as a functional dictator. This period, known as the Emergency, ended somewhat abruptly with Gandhi calling for new elections, which her party lost for the first time in Indian history. The victorious party, an alliance of several different

176 I THE REACTIONARY SPIRIT

opposition factions called the Janata Party, included leading members of the BJS (during the emergency, the RSS had been banned).

Though the RSS's adherents were forced to operate in conjunction with other opponents of the emergency, the group's core radicalism never truly disappeared. It represented an extreme response to what the Indian scholar Pratap Bhanu Mehta calls the "radical uncertainty" of life after democratization in India: the fundamental process of dissolving "old ways of instituting authority and recognizing identities" in favor of a more egalitarian vision of shared democratic citizenship. "The experience of democracy in India has opened up numerous points of dissent, new conflicts of values and identities, a permanent antagonism of meaning and interest that leaves its citizens often with an overwhelming sense that Indian society is flying off in many different directions at once," Mehta wrote in his book *The Burden of Democracy*.

In 1980, the RSS founded a new political arm designed to rally Hindus disturbed by these many social transformations under a new banner: the BJP. And it was this political formation that finally figured out how to sell Hindutva to a wider audience. The key was to find, Orbán-like, an issue that could gin up reactionary sentiments among the electorate. In the 1980s, the BJP hit on a gold mine: a fight between Hindus and Muslims over a 450-year-old mosque.

The Babri Masjid stood in the northern Indian city of Ayodhya, on a site that many Hindus believed to be the birthplace of Rama (the seventh avatar of the Hindu deity Vishnu). The dispute over who should control the site had been unresolved since 1949, when Hindus found a (reportedly planted) statue of Rama inside the mosque, but it took on new life in 1984, when Hindu nationalists began a campaign to demolish the mosque and replace it with a Hindu temple. This movement was largely coordinated by members of an extensive network of RSS-affiliated organizations, a collective called the Sangh Parivar (Sangh family). As the decade went on, and the anti-mosque movement gathered steam, the BJP turned the controversy into a centerpiece of its political rhetoric. The approach struck a chord: the party went from winning two seats in parliament in the 1984 election to winning eighty-five in 1989.

Around the same time, a separate conflict over caste wracked Indian politics. In 1990, the government pledged to implement the findings of a long-standing body called the Mandal Commission, a blue-ribbon panel tasked with studying caste divisions and proposing solutions. Its principal recommendation was to reserve 27 percent of higher-education admissions and public sector jobs for "other backward castes" beyond the Dalits. The backlash from upper-caste Hindus was fierce; the newspaper *India Today* wrote that the proposal caused a crisis "the likes of which has rarely engulfed the nation with such overwhelming intensity and rage." Roughly two hundred upper-caste university students set themselves on fire to protest the effect that the commission's recommendations would have on their future employability.

The BJP was actually a junior partner in the governing coalition during this fight, a fact that in theory committed it to supporting implementation of the Mandal Commission's suggestions. But the BJP leader L. K. Advani did something clever: he began a *yatra* (pilgrimage) to Ayodhya, explicitly billing it as an effort to unite Hindus in common cause. The message was that caste divisions were secondary to religious ones; Hindus should stop fighting amongst themselves over Mandal and instead focus on working together against the Muslims. It was the birth of "kamandal" politics—a term that typically refers to a water pot used by Hindu ascetics but in context means the use of Hindu nationalism to counteract the Mandal-era politics of caste.

Upper-caste Hindus saw the BJP as their best hope to block Mandal implementation. In the 1991 election, the BJP won 120 seats in parliament—second only to Congress. In 1992, a mob made up of RSS activists and BJP officials attacked the Babri Masjid after a speech by Advani. They tore it down.

The rise of the Indian reactionary spirit had begun.

NARENDRA MODI, REACTIONARY IN CHIEF

Advani's kamandal politics provided a reactionary synthesis for the Indian right. It linked Hindu nationalists, who opposed democratic equality on grounds that India should be a Hindu *rashtra* (state of the Hindus), with those upper-caste Hindu voters who opposed democratic equality because it threatened their privileged social standing and access to jobs. While Advani did not make the decisive reactionary move of mobilizing defenders of these hierarchies to attack democratic institutions, he showed that the raw potential for such a turn was there.

As the 1990s went on, and the BJP continued finding political success, it seemed to move away from the Hindutva extreme. After the party won a plurality of seats in the 1998 election, BJP leader Atal Bihari Vajpayee claimed the premiership, serving as prime minister between 1998 and 2004 (a position he had previously held for thirteen days in 1996). Vajpayee governed as a relative moderate, doing little to fundamentally undermine the secular constitutional order that the BJP theoretically aimed to undo. In 2006, the RSS formally repudiated Golwalkar's work.

The BJP's and RSS's moves to the center mirrored the global trend of far-right rhetorical accommodation to democracy, a shift made in India (as elsewhere) out of political exigency. In the 1990s and early 2000s, the BJP did not control a majority of seats in the Lok Sabha, the lower and more important house of parliament. It was thus forced to govern in coalition with parties that did not share its Hindu-nationalist ideals. Without overwhelming political power, taking a hard-line stance on equality and democracy could have meant political death.

Narendra Modi changed all that.

Modi is a lifelong believer in Hindutva. He joined the RSS in 1958, when he was eight years old. In 2001, he became chief minister of Gujarat, a large state on India's western coast. A year later, he presided over a horrific wave of communal riots in which at least 790 Muslims and 250 Hindus were killed. A senior Gujarati police officer would later testify that Modi told police to stand aside and allow Hindus to "vent their anger" on Muslim citizens.

In his book *Modi's India*, Jaffrelot described Gujarat as a "laboratory" for sharpening kamandal politics—for taking what Advani had started and turning it into a movement that could command outright national majorities. "Narendra Modi, because of his personal and political acumen, has succeeded where Advani failed," Jaffrelot wrote. "He invented a new style combining Hindu nationalism—his deep-rooted ideology—and populism."

In the 2014 national election, the BJP put forward Modi as its candidate for prime minister. The campaign focused not on Hindutva ideology but rather on economic development— Gujarat's economy had grown impressively under Modi's tenure as governor—and on corruption allegations against Congress. The BJP won an outright majority of seats in the Lok

Sabha, putting the coalitional concerns of the Vajpayee years in the rearview mirror.

Since Modi's ascent to power, he has attempted to make good on Hindutva ideology—becoming especially aggressive after his reelection in 2019, which followed a campaign waged explicitly on Hindu nationalism in the wake of an Islamist terror attack that killed upwards of forty Indian police officers. Following this victory, the BJP government passed a law creating a special pathway to citizenship for non-Muslim immigrants from nearby countries. It revoked the special self-governing status of Jammu and Kashmir, India's only Muslim-majority state and the subject of a bitter and violent territorial dispute with Pakistan. It edited history textbooks to remove references to Muslims' presence in India, a mention of Gandhi's killer being motivated by Hindu nationalism, and the use of the 2002 Gujarat riots as an example of the dangers of communal politics. The Mandal Commission's main recommendations remained unimplemented; Indian commentators spoke about the country entering a "post-Mandal" era.

The prime minister and his allies have directed never-ending invective at Muslims, creating a climate of hatred in which hate crimes against Muslims spiked dramatically. BJP leaders have, for example, promoted a conspiracy theory called "love jihad"—an alleged plot by Muslim men to marry Hindu women and convert them to Islam, with the ultimate goal of changing the country's demographics. This fearmongering has led at least eleven states to pass anti-"love jihad" legislation, which has been used to arrest Muslim men in interfaith relationships. In 2020, protests in Delhi against the discriminatory new immigration law were met with mob violence. Prior to the chaos, some members of the BJP were caught on camera directing chants of "shoot the traitors" against the protesters.

The Ayodhya movement won its final victory in 2020 when construction of a Hindu temple on the former site of the Babri Masjid began; Modi personally laid the ceremonial foundation stone.

Modi's agenda has been a wholesale Hindutva attack on Indian secularism—one he paired with a war on Indian democracy designed to ensure that there would be no roadblocks in his way. Modi's systematic dismantling of democratic guardrails was thus a textbook example of the reactionary spirit attacking democracy to protect social hierarchy. His high popularity throughout this process reflects an Orbán-like ability to use subtle legalistic maneuvering, a compelling personal story, and the popularization of a Schmittian ideology to mask a BJP assault on democracy. "The cult of Modi has led to the weakening, if not evisceration, of [several] crucial institutions that, in a democracy, are meant to hold unbridled power to account and to prevent the personalization of political power and the growth of authoritarianism," leading Indian historian Ramachandra Guha wrote in a 2022 essay.

Like Orbán, Modi has assailed the independence of election administration. To take one example, he has set up an "anonymous" donation system where the data on financial contributions is visible only to BJP apparatchiks in state-owned banks, leading to persistent BJP financial advantages over its rivals.

Like Orbán, Modi has systematically worked to seize control of the press, with Modi-friendly oligarchs now operating many of the leading outlets. In 2022, his (allegedly) corrupt billionaire ally Gautam Adani purchased a controlling stake in NDTV, one of India's oldest and most respected television outlets. The network's most prominent anchor, Ravish Kumar, quit in protest, citing the impossibility of covering the government impartially given an owner "whose success is seen to be linked to contracts granted by the government."

Like Orbán, Modi has politicized Indian law enforcement and regulatory agencies. Sedition prosecutions increased by 28 percent between 2014 and 2020; tax agencies have been weaponized against Modi's critics—including, in one high-profile case, the tax police going after a Modi-critical election commissioner's sister, wife, and son.

Like Orbán, Modi has defanged independent power centers. The Supreme Court has been cowed into going along with many of his policies, authorizing, among other things, the construction of the new Ayodhya temple. The prime minister has refused to appoint commissioners to the Central Information Commission, which handles government transparency requests. With this institution hamstrung, journalists and activists face difficulty finding out what his government is doing.

In at least one area, social media regulation, Modi has gone even further than Orbán, setting up a government agency empowered to review content-moderation requests, essentially a tool for coercing social media companies to take down speech Modi and the BJP don't like. This appears to have had an effect: seemingly at the government's request, X/Twitter blocked users in India from accessing over 120 prominent accounts in 2023, including those of an Indian MP and the leader of one of Canada's three major political parties (who is Sikh).

Canada, which is home to a large Indian diaspora (it actually has a larger Sikh population than India itself in percentage terms), has increasingly been drawn into conflict with backsliding India. In the fall of 2023, Canadian prime minister Justin Trudeau alleged that Indian agents had assassinated a Canadian citizen on Canadian soil—a Sikh man named Hardeep

Singh Nijjar whom the Indians had long accused of masterminding terrorist plots. India denied the allegations, but the Canadian government would not level such charges publicly without real evidence. The CBC, Canada's public broadcaster, reported that Canadian intelligence had intercepted "communications" in which Indian diplomats discussed the murder plot. The allegation blew up relations between the two democratic powers and created a massive headache for the United States, which needs to maintain close relations with both.

The evidence of India's autocratization has become increasingly undeniable. In 2021, V-Dem data showed that India was no longer a democracy, instead qualifying as what V-Dem calls an "electoral autocracy." Generally speaking, India experts thought that V-Dem was premature but picking up on a real trend: in Modi's second term, things had begun degrading fast.

If the BJP wins the 2024 elections, which seems likely as this book goes to press, India's democratic decline will assuredly continue. Pavithra Suryanarayan, the professor at London School of Economics who studies upper-caste support for the BJP, once told me that defeat of India's opposition parties in 2024 could mark the end of their national viability. Another five-year term would allow the BJP to cement political control over key government functions, giving it a potentially insurmountable advantage in future elections. This would complete the reactionary spirit's conquest of India—and turn the world's largest democracy into a version of Hungary.

"Winning creates its own dynamics—the way that parties are able to recruit their own candidates, to provide resources to win," she said. "From just a pure political point of view, this could be really hard [for the opposition] to overcome with just one more loss."

WHY INDIA AND AMERICA WILL DETERMINE
DEMOCRACY'S GLOBAL FATE

In 2024, both India and the United States will host elections that amount to referenda on the reactionary spirit. If Modi and Trump win, democracy will be in mortal peril in its two most important redoubts. Even if they lose, the threat from reactionary politics will not be over. We still live in an era when the democratic idea of equality is being pushed to new frontiers in ways that will surely provide fuel for more reactionary fires. So long as both the US government and the Indian government attempt to live up to their constitutional credos, influential segments of their populations will choose to reject democracy rather than accede to social equality, creating the raw political potential for future leaders in the mold of Trump and Modi.

This possibility forces us to contemplate the question, If one or both of the world's two largest democracies devolve into competitive authoritarianism, what will the future hold for democracy—not just in their borders, but around the world? The near-simultaneous collapse of democracy in two of its most important strongholds would be a worldwide event with few precedents. But based on what we know about global politics, it could represent an extinction-level threat to democracy everywhere.

In his book *Aftershocks*, University of Toronto political scientist Seva Gunitsky linked democracy's global rise and fall to changes in the distribution of global power. In times and places where authoritarian powers were ascendant, they tended to encourage imitators. During the Nazi rise in the Great Depression, fascist parties popped up around the world; in post–World War II Eastern Europe, Soviet power ensured communism's spread around the region. When democracies were relatively strong—as in Europe after World War I; western Europe and East Asia after World War II; or the entire world in the 1990s—the number of democracies across the planet tended to increase sharply.

Gunitsky argued that this was not an accident. The rapid rise or fall of great powers, which he terms "hegemonic shocks," tends to create an environment where systems of government can change with unusual speed. There are a few reasons for this phenomenon, but two are especially relevant to understanding the consequences of potential Indian and American authoritarianism: the influence of commerce and the power of example.

Wealthy countries tend to exert outsized influence on global politics. They can do this indirectly, by, for example, dominating popular culture; they can also do it directly, through things like sanctions on enemies and financial aid to friends. In the wake of a major power's decline or collapse, Gunitsky found, the end of its direct influence can imperil governments with similar regime types. "The Soviet collapse, for example, disrupted patronage networks throughout Africa in the early 1990s, undermining the basis of stable rule for many of the continent's despots," he wrote.

Hegemonic shocks also affect how much people *want* to live under certain forms of government. "By producing clear losers and winners, shocks legitimize certain regimes and make them more attractive to would-be imitators," Gunitsky argued. The end of the Cold War is again an instructive example. The failure of the Soviet Union so thoroughly discredited communism that its international advocates, once influential even in some democratic strongholds, lost nearly all meaningful support. Meanwhile, democratic capitalism started to look so attractive that revolutionaries around the world—even in places as repressive as China—attempted to bring it to their own countries.

Were India or the United States to become competitive authoritarian states, democracy's collapse would not likely be so dramatic as the Soviet Union's dissolution. Rather, it would be a continual slide away from competitive elections through incremental policy changes, one that would give leaders like Modi and Trump plausible deniability about what they were doing. Avatars of the reactionary spirit must, as we've seen, at least pretend to be democratic if they wish to successfully corrode an established democracy. Yet even such a veiled regime change in the United States and India could have significant implications for the global system, largely for the reasons Gunitsky suggests.

Since World War II, and especially since the end of the Cold War, the global economy has been governed by American rules. From American-led institutions like the World Bank to the dollar's status as reserve currency to the need for every country to maintain access to the behemoth American economy, America's economic primacy has defined global politics—requiring all countries to play by rules that advantage both democracies and prodemocracy forces inside authoritarian countries. The scholars Steven Levitsky and Lucan Way have shown that "linkage" to Western economies, meaning trade and political ties, creates powerful economic pressures for democratization and liberalizing reforms at home. During the large democratic wave following Soviet collapse, such linkages played an especially important role in the fall of some competitive authoritarian governments.

"Competitive authoritarian regimes in countries with extensive linkage to the West were exposed to intense international democratizing pressure during the post–Cold War period," Levitsky and Way wrote. "Where linkage was combined with substantial Western leverage, close scrutiny from the media, NGOs, and international organizations drew widespread attention to even relatively minor government abuses, which triggered—or threatened to trigger—costly punitive action by Western powers."

We can see how important this influence remains by looking at both Hungary and Israel. Hungary's economic model has long depended on the use and abuse of billions in European Union subsidies. Hungarian economist Rudolf Berkes attributed the entirety of his country's growth between 2012 and 2022 to EU support, telling NPR's *Marketplace* that it is "the one thing that keeps us from being poor and isolated." Orbán's regime also uses these funds to support his authoritarian political model, distributing them favorably to political allies to buy their support and ensure their market dominance relative to independent businesses. In late 2022, the EU suspended about 22 billion euros of this support in response to the increasingly undeniable evidence that democracy had collapsed in Hungary. For nearly a year, Orbán scrambled to convince EU leadership that he had made meaningful reforms without causing so much change that Hungary's competitive authoritarian system would become destabilized. By 2024, some—but not all—of Hungary's cash had been unfrozen.

Similarly, leading figures on the Israeli left have told me that their best hope for the occupation's end comes from outside pressure. They want the world's democracies, most notably the United States, to impose massive diplomatic and economic costs on the Israeli government if it continues to move in the direction of one-state apartheid. Even the credible threat of such moves, the Israeli left believes, would help wake up the

Israeli center to the necessity of undoing the occupation before it's too late.

Israel's and Hungary's alliances with democracies, and their integration into the global economy, have for now created levers that the international community can use to exert pro-democratic pressure. Reactionary forces in those countries are fully aware of this reality, and thus have to take it into account whenever they consider antidemocratic policies that are likely to draw the ire of democratic powers. But what would happen if the reactionaries had a free hand? We can see some signs by looking at China's rise. The world's second-largest economy has created an alternative market for countries seeking trade and aid with no human rights strings attached. If India, soon to be the world's third-largest economy, and the United States, its largest, fully succumbed to the reactionary spirit, the economic opportunities available to backsliders would be magnified considerably.

Whereas the American and Indian governments would appear much the same on the surface, they would in policy terms largely eschew the use of state power—including economic inducements—to defend and promote democratic equality abroad. The United States regularly uses its might in this fashion today, albeit inconsistently and haphazardly. India typically does not, but it had begun engaging in limited democracy promotion efforts prior to Modi's rise. Under the current government, the odds of India tossing its growing weight around to strengthen democracy elsewhere approximate zero.

Such a change to the global economy might not affect Hungary as much, given that the pressure on it primarily comes from the European Union. But it might have tremendous implications for Israel, a small but wealthy country that depends on access to global markets for its continued prosperity and on US aid for its defense needs. Instead of receiving *pressure* from the United States, Israel could get *legitimization*—as we saw in 2020, when the Trump administration proposed a "peace plan" that handed the Israeli right nearly everything it had wanted. Conversely, the Biden administration's unconditional support for Israel at the outset of the Gaza war gave way to a more nuanced and critical position as the death toll increased—especially when it came to ideas like "transferring" Palestinian civilians out of Gaza.

In addition to Israel, many other democracies around the globe would face an emboldened cadre of reactionaries in a world without the specter of democratic financial pressure. Recent events in Brazil, the world's third-largest democracy, make the potentially dire consequences plain. In the run-up to its 2022 presidential election, President Jair Bolsonaro—a reactionary who had previously praised Brazil's former military dictatorship—was laying the seeds for a Trump-like campaign to overturn the results, quite possibly extending all the way to a military coup. The plot was serious: the head of Brazil's navy was on board, and Bolsonaro's justice minister was carrying around a detailed plan for remaining in power in the event of Bolsonaro's defeat by his leftist rival, Luiz Inácio Lula da Silva.

These plots ultimately came to nothing, primarily because other Brazilians foiled them. But the United States also played an important role: a *Financial Times* investigation revealed that the Biden administration had waged an extensive campaign to deter the Brazilian elite from attacking the election results, threatening significant economic punishment. The American vow to suspend military aid and cooperation, which the Brazilian army relies on, were reportedly especially influential in deterring potential coup supporters from going along with Bolsonaro's plot. The United States had for once used its influence in Latin America to *stop* a right-wing coup.

But the disappearance of such economic statecraft is not the only, or even the most decisive, way that the rise of the reactionary spirit in the United States and India could influence democracy's future survival odds. There's also a crucial ideological component: simply by existing as nondemocratic states in a democratic guise, they could create a world in which democracy is much less likely to flourish outside their borders.

"America's most enduring contribution to the global spread of democracy has been *not* through its conscious efforts at democracy promotion, which have often been clumsy, inconsistent, and hypocritical, but through its exalted status as a model worthy of emulation and a side worth joining," Gunitsky wrote. "American power and success serves to legitimate the regime that it embodies and creates powerful incentives for leaders around the world to place themselves in the US camp."

Were the United States and India to succumb to the reactionary spirit, they would not weaken democracy by openly preaching the virtues of competitive authoritarianism. Instead, they would *change what democracy means* to many people around the world, showing that countries can succeed and even thrive through a system where "elected" authoritarians run roughshod over democratic norms in pursuit of power. "Democracy" would be redefined to include "illiberal democracy" of the Orbánist variety, scaling up his project of exporting Hungary's political model far beyond what Budapest could even dream of achieving otherwise.

America's ideological influence on global democracy is clear and requires little more elaboration. The power of India's example is less obvious, but still important—and will only become more so as the country continues its rapid economic and geopolitical ascent. Were Modi to succeed in remaking India into an authoritarian Hindutva state while the country continued to rise, it would become proof for many leaders in the Global South that Modi-style competitive authoritarianism works for countries like theirs—and that they could get away with building it at home without serious costs.

You can see inklings of this future in India's current public diplomacy. During a joint press conference with US secretary of state Antony Blinken in 2022, Indian external affairs minister Subrahmanyam Jaishankar defined the current government's "yardstick" for assessing a democracy's health as "the integrity of the democratic processes, the respect and credibility that they command with the people, and the non-discriminatory delivery of public goods and services." This is a weak definition of democracy: it contains no references to freedom of speech, freedom of the press, freedom of association, rights to due process, or any of the other myriad of things that prevent democratic governments from transforming themselves into competitive authoritarian regimes. It is a vision of democracy in which those who command an electoral majority can do whatever they want—regardless of whether they won that power majority in a truly fair election.

If India were to continue its rise while preaching this model of democracy, it would not need to engage in Orbán-like direct promotion of its new ideology to have a significant effect on other Global South countries. Success breeds imitators. Here, El Salvador's elected authoritarian Nayib Bukele is an instructive example.

When the sky-high Salvadoran murder rate dropped dramatically in 2023, following a harsh government crackdown on gangs that included the suspension of basic rights protections,

Bukele enjoyed a surge of popularity not only at home but in the Americas at large. In Guatemala, Honduras, and even Chile, pro-Bukele crowds took to the street to call for local implementation of his policies. Leading politicians in Costa Rica, Colombia, and Chile all cited him as a model to emulate. Even some prominent voices in the United States, like Senator Marco Rubio, joined in the pro-Bukele chorus. It might be quite difficult for foreign governments to actually emulate Bukele's crackdowns on democracy and human rights, but the fact that his model became so popular is a worrying sign for democracy in the Americas.

Bukele is far more nakedly autocratic than Modi; he ran for reelection in blatant violation of constitutional term limits and once literally ordered the army to occupy the Salvadoran congress. And El Salvador is, in geopolitical terms, orders of magnitude less significant than India—let alone the United States. If policy success under Bukele can breed admiration, imagine what the continued rise of India under permanent BJP rule might show the world.

The current direction of the United States and India is pushing democracy toward a much graver global crisis than it is already experiencing. In time, they might together turn competitive authoritarianism into a true ideological competitor to democracy—the first to emerge since the fall of the Berlin Wall.

WHY INDIA MATTERS MORE THAN CHINA

One might think that such Chinese state capitalism already poses such an ideological challenge to democracy. But so far, no real evidence suggests this is happening. There are no influential revolutionary movements looking to topple established democracies and install a Chinese-style state at home, nor any major political parties in those countries running on a platform of Xi Jinping Thought. This is in part because China has not really tried to present itself as an alternative. While it is perfectly willing to help authoritarian states that are in conflict with democracies, like Russia, it has devoted few resources to pushing its model around the world.

Perhaps that might change as China continues to rise—especially if the United States continues to decline. But challenging an existing global order is extremely hard. Part of the reason that the reactionary spirit has been so effective is that it avoids such a frontal ideological assault, instead cloaking itself in democratic ideas that already enjoy wide legitimacy.

For the Chinese model to become a true ideological threat to democracy, China itself would have to continue rising—proving, fairly conclusively, that it has built a better way to organize a society. It likely would need to become a global power on par with the United States, or at least become closer to one than it is at present.

There are significant reasons to believe it cannot. China's economic growth, the Communist Party's crowning achievement, has already slowed down dramatically in recent years. Larry Summers, the former US secretary of the Treasury, told the *Wall Street Journal* in 2022 that China's slowing growth increasingly suggests it will never overtake the United States as the world's largest economy as measured by gross domestic product (GDP). Pessimism about China's growth potential, once a fringe view, has become increasingly widespread among economists, with some saying that the full extent of China's economic woes are even worse than they seem. "The outside world underestimates how badly the Chinese economy is deteriorating," Desmond Shum, a prominent Chinese businessman, told the *New York Times*. "Many executives . . . say that staff are blatantly robbing and stealing from companies since the pandemic. Why? They have lost hope because the economic outlook is so bad."

Doubts about Chinese growth reflect not only some ugly economic data but also growing evidence of deeper problems in China's economic and political model. These fundamental issues give good reason to think China will never become strong enough to inspire a global challenge to democracy on par with the threat from the reactionary spirit's rise in India and America.

Start with demographics. Between 1980 and 2015, China maintained its infamous one-child policy, which strictly limited the size of most families to deal with population growth that the Communist Party felt was out of control. The policy was a catastrophic success: it did indeed bring China's birth rate down, but it also set up the nation for the greatest aging crisis in human history. By 2050, China's working-age population is likely to decline to around seven hundred million, while its elderly population will have risen dramatically, from roughly two hundred million in 2023 to five hundred million. Western democracies that face declining birth rates have been able to ameliorate the consequences for population growth via immigration. China, by contrast, has net-negative migration—meaning that more Chinese citizens leave than foreigners enter.

This puts the Chinese economy on the edge of a steep demographic cliff. With such a large population unable to work and yet still consuming resources, growth will necessarily slow dramatically. Increasingly, the state's budget will be consumed by pensions; fewer and fewer working-age Chinese will be contributing to its coffers via taxes. It's a recipe not only for a dramatic economic slowdown, but for a precipitous decline in the government's ability to support innovation and military spending.

Demographics may not even be China's biggest problem. For decades, the Chinese economic growth model has depended heavily on investment—meaning business and government spending on things like infrastructure. But this isn't sustainable; there are only so many roads and bridges you can build before they stop producing actual economic benefits. In the process of building all this unnecessary stuff, Chinese companies and governments have taken on dangerous amounts of debt—obligations they might not be able to pay given the uselessness of the projects their money is underwriting. A crash looms on the horizon.

For China's growth to move to a more sustainable footing, it needs to rebalance the economy toward consumption—meaning the sort of individual consumer purchases, such as eating out and buying goods like computers, that fuel growth in the world's highest-income societies. China's leadership has recognized this need in the past; it released a sixty-point rebalancing plan in 2013. But the effort has run into a major problem: the wealthy elites who benefit from the status quo, making fortunes by skimming government dollars or running state-owned enterprises, don't want things to change. The result has been very little successful rebalancing: investment still makes up around 43 percent of Chinese GDP, far higher than it should be in a consumption-based economy (the equivalent US figure is 21 percent).

Beginning sometime in the 2000s, China's debt levels began growing faster than its GDP—a sign that all the investment wasn't going toward productive growth. In fall 2021, the China Evergrande Group, one of the country's largest real estate corporations, missed a series of loan payments it could no longer afford to make. The immediate cause was a slowdown in real estate demand due to COVID. But Evergrande turned out to be the most-indebted large developer in the world, and it went into default. Evergrande's meltdown marked the beginning of an ongoing real estate crisis—nothing as dramatic as the 2008 financial crash, but a major market collapse nonetheless. The real estate meltdown is reverberating throughout the Chinese economy, putting major stress on local government finances and threatening to throw the country's banking system into crisis.

The politics of rebalancing are, if anything, getting worse. During the period of stratospheric economic growth in the 1990s and 2000s, China was a kind of party dictatorship: the president made policy decisions, but the Communist Party elite had ultimate authority—including the power to replace the president if they deemed it necessary. But current president Xi Jinping has centralized power in his own hands, transforming China into something more like a traditional "personalist" dictatorship, a system where one man, rather than a collective of party leaders, wields ultimate power (think Vladimir Putin's Russia). Xi's mistrust of power he can't control has reversed the economic liberalization trend that had contributed to prior decades of growth—and which, going forward, is essential to rebalancing. Many of Xi's key allies and loyalists are the leaders of state-owned enterprises who stand to lose the most from rebalancing, making reform even harder.

Xi's personalism isn't just an economic problem, as personalist regimes have a notorious habit of making grave errors in all sorts of policy areas. High-ranking officials tend to be incompetent yes-men, creating an inflexible government with major blind spots. It appears that this tendency really hurt China during the COVID-19 pandemic, when it stuck with the so-called zero-COVID policy—responding to outbreaks with extremely harsh lockdowns that trapped people in their homes—through the emergence of the extremely infectious Omicron variant. Xi's regime had been trumpeting zero-COVID as proof of his foresight and the superiority of China's political model to Western liberal democracy; they were entirely unwilling to consider changing course before it was too late. They had, for similar reasons, refused to engage in an adequate mass vaccination campaign. The most widely available vaccine was the homegrown Sinovac shot, which the government had promoted despite clear evidence that the Western equivalents performed markedly better.

The result was a two-front disaster. To maintain zero-COVID in the face of a more infectious variant, the government launched increasingly harsh crackdowns, at one point trapping most citizens of Shanghai, China's largest city, in their homes. Something in the Shanghai public cracked, producing mass protests in a city that had, in the past, lived well under the current regime. Similar protests against lockdowns erupted elsewhere, including in the capital, Beijing. When Xi finally ended zero-COVID, China's citizens were vulnerable to the worst consequences. Somewhere between 1 million and 1.5 million people died from the coronavirus in the first two months after zero-COVID.

The more China under Xi comes to resemble Putin under Russia, the more its economy will stagnate and the more likely it is to engage in policy blunders. And the worse things get, the more likely there is to be popular discontent with Communist Party rule. The Chinese regime has depended on an implicit bargain with its people: they sacrifice their freedoms in exchange for ever-improving living standards. The more that bargain breaks down, the more problems Xi's government will face on the home front.

This is not to say that Communist Party rule is doomed in China, or that China is bound to decline to a point of geopolitical irrelevance. It's the world's second-most-powerful country by a fairly wide margin, meaning that Beijing will almost certainly play a crucial role in global politics in the coming years. China's choices will help determine how bad climate change gets, what the future of global trade looks like, and whether there's a bloody war in East Asia waged over Taiwan or the South China Sea. The question of China, and Chinese–American relations in particular, remains a cardinal concern for twenty-first-century politics—even if China's rise is ending.

But there's a difference between being a great power, as China already is, and becoming a superpower rivaling the United States—the sort of country successful enough to inspire ideological copycats. China has not managed to do that so far, and it faces so many domestic problems that it seems incapable of doing it for the foreseeable future.

Things might be different if the United States decides to commit superpower suicide. "One clear lesson of past hegemonic shocks is that a sudden decline in American power poses a much greater challenge to global democracy than a gradual Chinese ascent," Gunitsky wrote in *Aftershocks*. "The future of democracy is tied to the future of American power."

There's no doubt that the likeliest scenario for dramatic American decline comes from domestic partisan politics. We have already seen three standoffs over the debt ceiling, where the threat of default and economic collapse was used as political leverage by House Republicans aiming to extract policy concessions from Democratic presidents. This kind of ruinous infighting, itself partially traceable to the baleful influence of the reactionary spirit, could cause severe damage to the foundations of America's relative power. The riots at the US Capitol on January 6, 2021, showed us that reactionary upheaval can produce destabilizing levels of civil violence. We have no idea how bad the next crisis will be if Trump narrowly loses the 2024 election—let alone what the consequences will be if he wins. The worse the crisis of American democracy gets, the easier it will be for China to sell its system as an attractive alternative.

The same is true, albeit to a lesser extent and on a different time horizon, with India. Today's India is not in China's class geopolitically, let alone America's. But it's already an important democratic exemplar, one that will likely emerge as a stronger model as it grows richer and more powerful. India's expanding role in the global economy and its increasing recognition as a standard-bearer for democracy will reshape the world in ways that we can't fully predict but that will likely matter enormously for democracy's long-term global survival prospects.

In his 1997 book *The Idea of India*, political scientist Sunil Khilnani argues that the founding of India is "the third moment in the great democratic experiment launched at the end of the eighteenth century by the American and French revolutions." In his view, it could prove more important than those momentous events:

> The Indian experiment is still in its early stages, and its outcome may well turn out to be the most significant of them all, partly because of its sheer human scale, and partly because of its location, a substantial bridgehead of effervescent liberty on the Asian continent. Asia is today the most economically dynamic region in the world, but it is also one where vast numbers of people remain politically subjugated.

Its leaders have confidently asserted that the idea and practice of democracy is somehow radically inappropriate and
intrusive to the more sober cultural manners of their people. The example of India is perhaps the most pointed challenge to these arguments.

Read today, Khilnani's analysis raises an unsettling question: What happens if this "bridgehead of effervescent liberty"
collapses under the weight of reactionary pressure?

CHAPTER 7

HOW
REACTIONARIES
LOSE

The reactionary spirit is, in a certain sense, inevitable. There is no way to prevent moves to social equality from emerging democratically, and no way to ensure that some portion of the population won't react to those moves by rejecting democracy itself. But the reactionary spirit's strength can vary dramatically. In many places and times, hierarchy has come under threat in a democracy without yielding a major backlash.

Take modern Canada. In the late twentieth century, the Canadian government abandoned a racist approach to immigration—colloquially called the "White Canada" policy—and welcomed an unprecedented influx of immigrants from around the world. About 23 percent of current Canadians were born outside its borders, the highest percentage in any wealthy democracy.

Yet Canada has also been persistently, perhaps even uniquely, resistant to the far-right surge that has swept the rest of the West. When a far-right protest occupied the streets of Ottawa for nearly a month in 2022, polls showed widespread disapproval of the protesters' actions from the Canadian people. One of this movement's allies, MP Pierre Poilievre, subsequently won the center-right Conservative Party's leadership—a worrying sign given his flirtation with conspiracy theories and proposal to defund the English-language side of the CBC, Canada's public broadcaster. But Poilievre is less radical than he seems: he supports Canada's permissive immigration policy, a striking contrast with nearly every far-right movement in a peer Western country. And there's little evidence that he would govern as an antidemocratic reactionary along the lines of a Trump or Modi.

This neutered extremism reflects decades of policy choices, including, but going far beyond, the country's decision to give high-skill foreigners preference in immigration. Since 1971, the Canadian government has worked extensively to turn multiculturalism into a central part of Canadian national identity. Policies like extensive educational reforms and financial support for minority inclusion have produced a country singularly comfortable with the decline of white Christian social dominance. A 2019 poll found that 62 percent of Canadians think multiculturalism has been "good" or "very good" for Canada. One academic study found that Canadians who express high levels of patriotism are actually more likely to support immigration, the opposite of every other country the researchers studied.

I spend a lot of time in Canada—my wife is from there—and tolerance-as-national-identity is something you can see on the ground. The country is hardly perfect; its housing market is among the most expensive in the world, which (per a 2023 survey) has led some Canadians to become more skeptical of immigration than they had been in the past. But the degree to which diversity has become a public value, one shared across the political mainstream and made visible in everyday life, has no parallel in any other country I've visited. By putting the weight of the state and mainstream political parties behind a commitment to equality, Canada vaccinated itself against the reactionary spirit, leading to a much weaker infection than can be found in other Atlantic democracies.

For some time, I wasn't sure what useful lessons other countries could draw from the Canadian model. Canada's sense of national identity was relatively weak prior to the 1970s, creating room for a kind of nation-building project centering tolerance and diversity. This project took decades of work, making it impractical as a short-term solution to a reactionary crisis. But in November 2022, I had a conversation with an American politician—Adrian Fontes, the newly elected Arizona secretary of state—that led to an epiphany.

Fontes, an attorney, served in the Marine Corps as a marksmanship instructor. He's a former elections supervisor in Maricopa County—one of the most important counties in one of America's swingiest states—and is also an accomplished mariachi singer. In a phone call, he told me he wanted to add "butcher" to his long list of careers and hobbies ("People gotta eat," he said). The week prior to our conversation, Fontes had narrowly pulled out a victory in his campaign for secretary of state, Arizona's top election-supervision job. It was a race with extremely high stakes; his opponent, Republican Mark Finchem, was a member of the Oath Keepers militia who had participated in the January 6 rally. If someone like Finchem were in charge of elections in such a pivotal state, the odds of a crisis in the 2024 elections would have gone up exponentially.

Yet Fontes beat him. And to hear him tell it, the reason for his win was "not too complicated": he campaigned in defense of American democracy against the wild allegations against it, and voters responded.

"Voters are just tired of the bullshit. They know it's non-sense, that there's no evidence behind the big lie or any of that stuff, and they rejected it," he said. "This isn't winning-candidate blowhard arrogance. I'm talking confidence in the American ethos, a continuous but bumpy [democratic] march forward."

Fontes wasn't alone in taking this approach. Across the country, Democratic candidates facing election denialists put the defense of democracy front and center in their messaging. President Biden devoted a high-profile speech in October, dubbed the Democratic Party's "closing argument," to the topic. It seems to have worked: in every swing state across the country, Republican candidates for governor and secretary of state who rejected the outcome of the 2020 election lost their bids in 2022.

To find out if democracy really was a decisive argument in those races, as Fontes suggested, I interviewed a number of candidates who'd beat election deniers and the strategists who'd helped the winners craft their message. They all said that the democracy message, the defense of the nonpartisan foundational principles of the American system, broke through—and the numbers seem to back them up. Exit-poll data revealed that democracy and Republican extremism were two of voters' top priorities in the 2022 election. A 2023 analysis from Catalist, the gold-standard Democratic data firm, found that candidates who embraced election denial suffered a one- to four-point penalty when compared with other Republicans.

This democracy strategy worked, I realized, for basically the same reason Canada has proven so resistant to the reactionary onslaught: because it appeals to the country's fundamental self-identity. Much like Canada has built an identity around multiculturalism, America has long grounded its identity—what Fontes called the "American ethos"—around democracy. When prodemocracy candidates are able to show that reactionaries are in fact opposed to democracy, by pointing to their unhinged rhetoric on the topic, they should be able to win over a significant number of voters.

The best way to defend a democracy, I've realized, is to *say you're defending a democracy*. Democracies under attack don't need to build a whole new national ethos like Canada did. They just need to double down on the one they have.

In the past several years, we've seen this strategy used to frustrate and even defeat reactionaries around the world. Jair Bolsonaro lost his 2022 reelection bid in Brazil in large part due to the opposition's credible claim to be defending Brazilian democracy against Bolsonaro's attacks. Israelis' concerns about democracy in their country led to Netanyahu's brief dethronement from 2021 to 2022 and were at the heart of the (partially) successful protest movement against his judicial overhaul. Czech prime minister Andrej Babiš, who had displayed disturbing Orbán-like tendencies after taking office in 2017, subsequently lost both a parliamentary and a presidential election—with the threat to Czech democracy playing a role both times. In October 2023, a group of Polish opposition parties defeated the reactionary PiS government, despite laws that ensured the PiS party would be playing on a favorably tilted field. During the campaign, opposition standard-bearer

Donald Tusk led a five-hundred-thousand-person prodemocracy march in Warsaw; after the first exit polls previewed his
victory, Tusk announced, "Democracy has won!"

The vulnerability of the reactionary spirit stems, somewhat ironically, from one of its greatest strengths: its capac-
ity to operate within democracy's ideological confines. When
the reactionary spirit's modern avatars claim to be defending
democracy, they are implicitly conceding that democracy is
worth defending. The more a citizenry is convinced that reactionary parties are actually enemies of democracy, the harder
it will be for those parties to win power. And because reactionary movements are in fact antidemocratic, they will necessarily do antidemocratic things, providing evidence democracy's
defenders can use to press the case.

Calling out the deception at the heart of reactionary politics is not a foolproof strategy. Canny authoritarians like
Orbán, Netanyahu, and Modi all have employed various
means for avoiding backlash—hiding their antidemocratic
policies behind a complex technical-legal veneer or shift-
ing public debate to their favored polarizing identity-related
topics. The effect of these tactics depends critically on local
circumstances—for example, on the skill of leaders and activists on both the pro- and the antidemocratic sides. There is no
"one neat trick" for defeating the reactionary spirit.

But the past few years have shown us that tackling democratic backsliding head-on can, if done correctly, rally a
winning coalition to democracy's defense. And a growing
body of evidence demonstrates what "done correctly" actually looks like. New statistical research and case studies from
across the globe provide specific, actionable guidance for politicians, activists, philanthropists, and ordinary citizens who
wish to come to democracy's defense. This kind of immediate

action is necessary not only to protect democracy in the short term but to lay the groundwork for more fundamental changes—like abolishing the Electoral College in the United States or ending the occupation in Israel—that currently seem impossible due to the electoral strength of reactionary forces.

The reactionary spirit is strong, drawing its power from some of the most fundamental forces in human psychology and culture. But democracy and its underlying ideal of equality also have deep roots. They speak to something fundamental about the way humans imagine themselves and the societies they live in. And it turns out that when democracy is in danger, people are more than willing to act to defend it.

DEMOCRACY'S ANTIBODIES

The reactionary spirit wins support by weaponizing exclusion: uniting an "us" committed to maintaining the current inequality against an existentially threatening "them." Yet small-*d* democrats aim to build a different kind of political society. True democracy becomes stable, in the sense of commanding enough public support to remain in place indefinitely, by uniting the polity through *inclusion*. To understand how this is even possible, we must turn to the greatest democratic theorist of the twentieth century: John Rawls.

Philosophers often credit Rawls's 1971 masterwork, *A Theory of Justice*, with single-handedly reviving the moribund study of political philosophy in the English-speaking world. Despite his towering influence, he shunned the limelight, refusing interview requests from the media and almost never speaking or writing for a general audience. Although the sheer ingenuity of Rawls's thought has attracted some public commentary over time, his influence has been felt primarily in the academy rather than the wider world.

There are reasons for this beyond Rawls's reclusiveness. His work consists of a series of intricate, interlocking concepts with clunky-sounding names that don't lend themselves to pithy quotation. Moreover, his writing focuses primarily on what he called "ideal theory": imagining what a just democratic system would look like under reasonably favorable conditions. In a world where democracy faces conditions that are far from favorable, such an exercise might feel like a utopian extravagance.

But Rawls's thought also contains useful, even actionable insights into democracy's moral heart. His 1993 book *Political Liberalism* in particular attempts to answer a question of immense practical importance: How can democracy become stable when its citizens disagree so fundamentally on basic moral and religious issues? His answer, read properly, can help us understand when and how the reactionary spirit loses.

Rawls argued that democratic stability arises from a kind of political alignment among the bulk of citizens, which he called an "overlapping consensus." This is a general agreement, tacit rather than explicit, on a set of political ideas that serve as the foundations for political debate. In a democracy, all kinds of people can agree that things like equality and freedom are important—even as they disagree on the *reasons* such things are important. American Jews, for example, might endorse freedom as a political value based on their own history of persecution and their reading of the story of the Exodus; secular conservatives might see freedom as an important pillar of America's founding tradition.

People coming from these different perspectives will certainly have disagreements about what values like freedom mean in practice. That's fine for Rawls, even healthy—so long as those disputes are resolved through the electoral system. What really matters is that people agree on a reasonably democratic set of bedrock values, ones that ensure that their remaining disagreements can be handled through peaceful electoral means.

This may sound unrealistic, and in some ways it is. Rawls's system assumes a degree of unanimity on tough moral questions that's likely unattainable in most countries. But if you strip away his grandest ambition and focus on the most fundamental aim of the overlapping consensus—the construction of stable and widespread agreement surrounding essential ideas of political democracy—a real-world overlapping consensus starts to look more plausible.

Survey data has shown, again and again, that people in democracies around the world believe they have a fundamental right to choose who leads them. A 2021 paper in the journal *Democratization*, for example, examined data on how people in ten European nations felt about "populist radical right" parties in their country. Researchers found that, in the countries surveyed, "there is a constituency of roughly half [the] electorate that dislikes this party family and strongly supports liberal democracy despite its dissatisfaction with the ways in which the democratic regime is working." Moreover, a meaningful number of far-right supporters expressed support for democracy as the best available governing system—meaning that such factions don't have the strength to attack democracy openly (presuming they want to).

This consensus on democracy is reflected in the way people and democratic countries talk and argue about politics. There's often an assumption in public rhetoric and writing, one not even stated but simply taken for granted, that citizens care about democracy in their country and want it to flourish. This is evidence of an overlapping consensus in action. To see what I mean, it's helpful to look at a specific example—the *New York Times*'s widely circulated 1619 Project.

The project's central conceit, that the first year slaves arrived on American shores should be considered a founding date on par with 1776, has been described in some quarters as an assault on the American democratic tradition. But the project's lead essay, by Nikole Hannah-Jones, is actually an argument for why Black people, despite their long history of oppression, should still take pride in America and its democracy. For Hannah-Jones, the history of Black struggle for equality gives her community an ownership stake in American democracy.

"Black Americans have also been, and continue to be, foundational to the idea of American freedom. More than any other group in this country's history, we have served, generation after generation, in an overlooked but vital role: It is we who have been the perfecters of this democracy," she wrote. "No one cherishes freedom more than those who have not had it. And to this day, black Americans, more than any other group, embrace the democratic ideals of a common good."

What has struck some as a radical Black-nationalist critique of the American state—a root-to-branch effort to overturn the country's founding mythology—is actually an argument for *loyalty* to that state and for faith in its democracy. Because "the year 1619 is as important to the American story as 1776," Hannah-Jones wrote, "no people has a greater claim to [the] flag than us."

This is the Rawlsian vision of democratic stability at work. Hannah-Jones is a fairly radical Black critic of the American state, but this worldview led her to embrace democracy's core principles rather than reject them. Hannah-Jones and others who share her view have entered into an overlapping consensus with millions of their fellow Americans, each of whom ended up endorsing the same values for different reasons rooted in their own backgrounds and convictions. Despite Americans' different religious and moral belief systems—what Rawls called "comprehensive doctrines"—they've still managed to find a certain amount of common ground on democracy's essential ideals. It's a kind of agreement that, Rawls argues, should be able to build on itself over time: "gradually, as the success of political cooperation continues, citizens gain increasing trust and confidence in one another."

Crucially, an overlapping consensus needs only to include "reasonable" people who hold "reasonable" comprehensive doctrines. Supporters of reasonable doctrines can agree to cooperate with others on mutually agreeable political terms; adherents to unreasonable doctrines, by contrast, seek to force their ideas on others who are "dominated or manipulated, or under the pressure of an inferior political or social position." People gripped by the reactionary spirit are, by this Rawlsian definition, "unreasonable": they aim to undermine democracy for the express purpose of coercing those lower on the social hierarchy to accept their inferior position.

Rawls assumed, for the purposes of his idealized system, that the number of such "unreasonable" people would be small and politically insignificant. He acknowledged that if this assumption doesn't hold, democratic stability might start to buckle. The closest he came to suggesting how to prevent such a collapse is in a cryptic footnote on page sixty-four of *Political Liberalism*: "That there are doctrines that reject one or more democratic freedoms is itself a permanent fact of life, or seems so. This gives us the practical task of containing them—like war and disease—so that they do not overturn political justice."

This note may seem, on first blush, like a devastating concession to Schmitt. Rawls appears to be admitting that politics is ultimately about defining friends and enemies, with "unreasonable" people taking on the role of the enemy who must be destroyed. But if we read more carefully, Rawls isn't saying that anyone needs to be exiled from the political community—let alone killed, as Schmitt believed enemies could and perhaps should be. The problem for Rawls isn't a particular group of people at all, but rather the popularity of a set of *beliefs*. Those beliefs do not need to be eradicated—he explicitly says that this is likely impossible—but rather "contained." Such containment is a political task, much like preventing wars or managing disease outbreaks, that can and should be handled through normal democratic means. The appropriate response is not abandoning the idea of an overlapping consensus on democracy, but marshaling democracy's resources to limit the ability of unreasonable actors to destroy it.

The very existence of an overlapping consensus suggests how that can work: by mobilizing the people inside the consensus to act on their democratic faith. If a majority of citizens are basically reasonable in the way Rawls suggests, then they care about democracy for reasons rooted in their most deeply held beliefs and identities. And if that's the case, then there's a potent reservoir of public sentiment that can be activated when citizens believe democracy to be under threat.

Rawls's overlapping consensus thus helps us see how the old cliché "diversity is our strength" can be true. Democracy's commitment to including *all* people—to taking diversity seriously and allowing every citizen to engage in politics on their own terms—is what turns people into loyal democratic citizens. Democracies persist because they command authentic support from free people for reasons that actually mean something to them. They attain, in Rawls's phrasing, "stability for the right reasons."

Preserving this stability may well require changing laws and reforming institutions, but that's an endpoint rather than a beginning. Such changes are difficult to accomplish in the midst of a reactionary convulsion; they require that reactionary sentiment be well enough contained that prodemocratic forces can win sufficient political power to implement their reforms democratically. The first step down that path is activating the overlapping consensus: convincing a critical mass of reasonable people that democracy is in fact in danger and in need of defense. And indeed, we have seen several recent elections where this kind of appeal to the overlapping consensus has been decisive.

In Brazil's 2022 election, the leading candidate challenging Bolsonaro—the former two-term president Luiz Inácio Lula da Silva, widely known as Lula—was a left-wing firebrand, a harsh critic of economic inequality and of US policy toward Latin America. To attract voters in the Brazilian center, swing voters who might decide the election, Lula emphasized the contrast between the democratic Brazil during his terms and the country's increasingly authoritarian drift under Bolsonaro. In his campaign kickoff speech, he asked voters to choose between "the Brazil of democracy or authoritarianism [and] the Brazil of knowledge and tolerance or the Brazil of obscurantism and violence."

Lula failed to receive an outright majority in the first round of the election, leading to a second-round runoff with Bolsonaro. The endorsement of the third-place candidate—a center-right senator named Simone Tebet—became crucial.

Could she really pick Lula, whom she had previously accused of being corrupt, over an incumbent president who shared her right-wing values on issues like abortion?

The answer was yes, and democracy was the reason.

"I maintain my criticism of Luiz Inácio Lula da Silva," Tebet said in her endorsement speech. "But I will give him my vote, because I recognize his commitment to democracy and the constitution, which I have never seen from the current president."

Tebet's endorsement may well have been decisive. Pre-election polls suggested that at least 70 percent of her supporters—amounting to roughly 2.8 percent of the total electorate—switched to Lula in the second round. He ended up beating Bolsonaro by a 1.8-point margin, meaning that Lula very likely would have lost without the Tebet bloc. Lula's ability to tap into the Brazilian overlapping consensus, to use democracy as a political bridge to reach politicians and voters who disagreed with him on fundamental issues, is a major reason why he—and not the reactionary Bolsonaro—is president today.

After Lula's victory, Bolsonaro attempted to contest the elections and plot a coup—but could not build support among the Brazilian conservative elite for such a brazen move. On January 8, 2023, Bolsonaro supporters attacked government buildings in the capital, Brasília, in an attempt to put him back in power. They were not only put down but rejected across the political mainstream. Over the course of the next year, Brazilian police arrested over two thousand rioters; Brazil's electoral court disqualified Bolsonaro from holding office for eight years without the sort of intense partisan controversy that surrounded similar moves against Trump in the United States. A December 2023 poll found that 89 percent of Brazilians viewed the violent uprising unfavorably. On January 8, 2024, Lula hosted a "Democracy Unshaken" event in Brasília attended by a who's who of the Brazilian political elite—a testament to the fact that the country's democracy "seems to have recovered," as political analyst Brian Winter put it.

In Brazil and elsewhere, people really are motivated by loyalty to democracy. They see it as an expression, in part, of their own personal ideas about what a good life and a good society look like. They care to the point where they are willing to march and vote and engage in the endless tedium of phone calls and door knocking that make up electoral politics, because their lives and histories are bound up with living in a democratic society. The commitment to democracy might have felt especially urgent in Brazil, where an authoritarian regime had ruled within living memory, but it also applies in some of democracy's longer-standing redoubts.

In her 1619 Project essay, Hannah-Jones wrote of her father's decision to fly an American flag outside her childhood home, something she couldn't understand as a young girl who was acutely aware of the brutality and discrimination Black people had always faced in the United States. But as she learned more, she aged into a kind of American patriot: "Like most young people, I thought I understood so much, when in fact I understood so little. My father knew exactly what he was doing when he raised that flag. He knew that our people's contributions to building the richest and most powerful nation in the world were indelible, that the United States simply would not exist without us."

Versions of this sentiment exist everywhere democracy does. Its power is why reactionaries are so afraid to attack the idea of democracy head-on. Defeating reactionaries means engaging in the hard work of winning elections, of trying to break through profound social and ideological divisions in places like the United States and Brazil by convincing a decisive number of voters that democracy truly is on the line. It means building a robust civil society that can sustain the overlapping consensus—organizing in defense of it in times of trouble and strengthening it in times of peace.

It means not just talking about democracy, but actually *doing* it.

WHEN REACTIONARY ERRORS LEAD
TO DEMOCRATIC VICTORIES

Activating voters' support for democracy is not just a simple matter of screaming, "Democracy is under attack!" as loudly as one can. If it were that easy, reactionary candidates would never win elections. The question for politicians is how to get citizens to believe there's a real threat—one scary enough that they need to donate their precious free time and energy to combating it.

Cases of democratic backsliding around the world suggest that there are moments in time when it becomes a lot easier to do that. Those windows of opportunity are often created by the reactionaries themselves.

The modern reactionary project has a basic problem: it needs to undermine democracy without *appearing* to do so. Throughout this book, we've seen authoritarian factions inside democracies employ some combination of three broad strategies to thread this needle. They enact technical and complex antidemocratic policies that ordinary citizens don't notice or understand. They polarize the population along ethnoreligious lines so severely that citizens overlook antidemocratic actions.

And they claim that they are "merely" attacking liberalism rather than democracy to justify curtailing basic democratic freedoms.

Each of these strategies demands a lot from reactionary politicians. They require tricky judgment calls about whether a policy is sufficiently technical to escape notice, whether a piece of antiminority rhetoric will attract more people than it will turn off, and whether the particular liberal ideas and values they assail are really that unpopular. Reactionaries often make the wrong choices in these areas; in fact, it's almost inevitable that they will. Even the savviest reactionaries don't have perfect knowledge about how elites or the public will react to their decisions. These mistakes often have the effect of dramatizing their true goal—exposing in an especially clear way that they are, in fact, attacking democracy. When that happens, at least some people can be woken up to what's really going on in their country.

An isolated misstep may generate only limited resistance. But a series of errors, or an especially egregious one, might create an opportunity for something much bigger: a moment ripe for what political scientists Murat Somer, Jennifer McCoy, and Russell Luke termed "transformative repolarization," a change in the fundamental dynamics that define political conflict in a country.

The concept of transformative repolarization came out of a 2021 paper that assessed the evidence for a variety of different strategies for fighting democratic backsliding. Repolarization works, Somer and colleagues argue, by presenting voters with "a binary choice over democracy or justice without demonizing the 'Other'"—that is, by reframing the terms of the debate between democracy and inclusion on the one hand, and those who would threaten it on the other. A political movement attempting this maneuver does not turn its rivals' supporters into Schmittian enemies, but rather portrays itself as open to anyone who supports democracy—even former supporters of a reactionary faction. Democracy serves as an overarching narrative that binds people in a society together, despite their prior disagreements, to act in defense of fair elections and political cooperation. It's a very Rawlsian idea.

Political parties, activists, and even ordinary citizens can do the work of transformative repolarization immediately in the wake of an authoritarian misstep. They can use the opportunity to defeat a major threat to democracy or even to begin undoing the damage that's already been done. The key thing is to identify the specific political arguments and tactics that work in a given context to expose the authoritarian overreach in question and reorient politics around democracy's defense. The 2022 US midterm elections show what this looks like in practice.

In 2021, it had seemed as if democracy was a losing political cause. Despite the fact that the year began with rioting at the US Capitol on January 6, there was little evidence that ordinary Americans perceived increasing reactionary radicalism to be a threat to the democratic system. One poll, conducted in October of that year, found that over twice as many Republicans as Democrats (seventy-one to thirty-five) believed that democracy in America was facing a "major threat"—indicating that Republicans had come to believe Trump's lies about a stolen election, while Democrats didn't understand the threat those lies posed to American democracy's future.

By the time the midterm elections were held a year later, things had changed. Data from the AP VoteCast showed that

56 percent of Democrats said the future of democracy was their "primary consideration" at the ballot box, compared with just 34 percent of Republicans. What happened?

The repolarization started when the GOP's reactionary wing overreached. Across the country, Republicans nominated especially extreme election deniers in highly visible swing state races. These candidates, through their own statements and actions, embodied the reactionary spirit in especially blatant and undeniable terms. Tim Michels, the GOP candidate for governor in Wisconsin, vowed that Republicans "will never lose another election" in the state if he won.

The question for democracy's defenders—in this case, Democrats and their allies—was how to take advantage of the overreach. Their private polling uncovered something important: that arguments about democracy worked best as part of a general argument about extremist attacks on "freedom."

The crucial additional event was the US Supreme Court's summer 2022 decision in *Dobbs v. Jackson*, which overturned *Roe v. Wade*—a highly visible ruling that put legal abortion, supported to some degree by a fairly large majority of Americans, back on the ballot. As it happens, the same candidates who argued that the 2020 election was stolen *also* tended to endorse strict limitations on abortion. By connecting abortion and democracy in a general narrative of extremist attacks on freedom, Democrats found a way to make the threat to democracy feel real and immediate to voters.

Generally, these kinds of nitty-gritty campaign messaging choices don't matter all that much. But 2022 was a very weird election. Democrats performed poorly in many races, in line with the historical pattern of the incumbent president's party losing seats in midterm elections, but did unusually well in swing states and close elections. This was especially common when Democrats faced candidates who were *both* election deniers and hardline pro-lifers. In Georgia, for example, Republican governor Brian Kemp—who had enacted a strict six-week abortion ban but defended the legitimacy of the 2020 election—handily beat Democratic challenger Stacey Abrams. But in the US Senate race, incumbent Democrat Raphael Warnock narrowly defeated the more radical Republican candidate, Herschel Walker, who both opposed abortion and had previously claimed that the 2020 election was stolen.

The entanglement of two key issues, democracy and abortion, makes it hard to assess which one was *more* important. But data analyses have generally, albeit not universally, found that election denial mattered in particular. One of the most rigorous of the examinations, from Stanford University political scientists Andrew Hall and Janet Malzahn, concluded that candidates who denied the results of the 2020 election suffered a roughly 2.3-point penalty relative to other Republicans. This might seem like a small number, but it was big enough to cover the margin in tight races like those in Georgia. In an interview for Stanford's website, Hall explained that this margin could very well have significant implications for future elections:

> The results suggest pretty strongly you don't want to nominate someone for president or any other major office in 2024 who's making this election-denying stuff a big part of their focus because it's really unpopular with this important set of swing voters. Those swing voters are going to matter and these races tend to be quite close. If you look at the strategies that candidates and parties take, they're looking at optimizing a quarter of a percentage point. So to

tell them that there's this delta that's potentially more than two percentage points, that's a huge deal. Strategically, if you care about winning elections, I think the takeaway's pretty clear that nominating these kinds of candidates is not a good strategy.

In this way, the 2022 US midterms offered a story similar to the one illustrated by the Brazilian presidential election: although many issues mattered in both elections, democracy arguments managed to reach a small but decisive bloc of persuadable voters.

There are two other important lessons from the American case for doing transformative repolarization. First, the nature of a country's overlapping consensus matters quite a lot. For Rawls, an overlapping consensus is not merely an agreement on the idea of holding elections; it's a general alignment on a set of political values. From the founding of the United States, freedom has been one of the values—if not the *central* value—guiding how Americans think. Jen Fernandez Ancona, a Democratic strategist who helped to develop the freedom message, told me that her thinking was informed by both this basic insight and the polling supporting it, which found that freedom was the political value that Americans said mattered most to them by a fairly wide margin. Connecting democracy to another core value like freedom in the overlapping consensus helps engage more people.

Of course, "freedom" is no more a magic word than "democracy." Merely saying that your opponent opposes either will not guarantee a victory or even necessarily move many voters. When we talk about this kind of political messaging advice, we're talking about moving fractions of percentage points of voters—and that happening only after extensive repetition of carefully planned arguments in stump speeches, debates, and political advertising.

But even small percentages may be enough. Democracies facing a surge in the reactionary spirit often have narrowly divided electorates, meaning every bit of persuasion matters. This kind of rhetorical fine-tuning may seem to matter only at the margins, but *elections are often won at the margins*. A fractional shift can be enough to make the difference between a reactionary holding a critical office and losing. Kari Lake, the hard-line election denier who ran for Arizona governor, lost by seven-tenths of a percentage point.

The second lesson is that prodemocracy political leaders need to identify how their struggles are *linked* to other issues that matter to key portions of the electorate. For some voters, prodemocracy arguments can feel abstract and disconnected from their real-life concerns. But if something they already care about can be connected to democracy, the consequences of antidemocratic political drift can feel more real. Consider the way the prodemocracy factions handled abortion in the United States and Brazil. In America, extensive polling suggested that *Roe v. Wade* was popular—and that by moving swiftly to outlaw abortion after its fall, Republicans had created a major vulnerability for themselves on a vital issue. In that context, tying democracy to abortion made all the sense in the world, especially given the way they could be put together under the "freedom" umbrella.

But in Brazil, where abortion is outlawed and roughly 80 percent of the population is Catholic or evangelical, things were different. When Lula endorsed legal abortion during the campaign, he faced significant pressure and had to backtrack (somewhat). Had Lula tied his democracy message to abortion in the American fashion, he would have risked alienating key swing constituencies—including Tebet, whose endorsement proved so crucial. Instead, Lula found other ways to make democracy arguments feel more concrete, sometimes by connecting the idea of democracy to his core messages surrounding economic equality and shared prosperity. "The Brazilian people want to live well, eat well, have a good home," he said in his victory speech. "This is how I understand democracy. Not just as a beautiful word written in law, but as something tangible, that we feel in our skin, and that we can build in everyday life."

Such linkages can yield success in even the most unfriendly environments. In the 2019 Budapest mayoral election, opposition candidate Gergely Karácsony campaigned on a message that combined democracy and housing, arguing that the previous nine years of Fidesz political hegemony lay at the root of the sky-high cost of living in Hungary's capital. Karácsony won, in what remains Fidesz's most significant electoral defeat since Orbán began building his competitive authoritarian regime in 2010.

The underlying message here, more than anything else, is that democracy's defenders need to be nimble. They need to be on guard for the inevitable reactionary overreaches, assess their significance, and then attack relentlessly when opportunity strikes, using a message tailored to the specific time and place where they're campaigning. Linkage strategies can strengthen such a message, potentially even creating opportunities against reactionaries like Orbán in 2019, who hadn't obviously tripped up.

Defeating the reactionary spirit at the ballot box depends at least in part on exposing reactionaries for who they really are. The tactics may vary, but political leaders need to start with a sense that enough people who live in democracies really care about continuing to do so—and that they can't be duped forever.

HOW YOU—YES, YOU—CAN HELP SAVE DEMOCRACY

Any serious set of proposals for addressing democratic erosion must go beyond advice for candidates and campaigns. In part, this is because politicians and parties do not determine the outcome of elections alone. Such contests are decided by the sum total of actions of millions of citizens involved in the democratic process through voting, volunteering, and the like. Activists, donors, journalists, human rights groups, and ordinary citizens all have real power to shape the ultimate outcome.

Nonpoliticians have the potential to do more than merely block reactionary action or aid in the contest for power. In democratic and even some competitive authoritarian contexts, citizens can take actions that address the root causes of the reactionary spirit's rise, getting involved in ways that strengthen the prodemocratic overlapping consensus, build organizational capacities for pushback against reactionary overreach, and even change people's core values relating to democracy and hierarchy.

To illustrate how this works, it's helpful to turn to a third successful appeal to an overlapping consensus: the 2023 Israeli protests against Netanyahu's judicial overhaul. The movement itself grew out of an authoritarian overreach—specifically, the public revelation that the prime minister had (allegedly) attempted to suborn the media. There had been a wave of anti-Netanyahu protests in 2019 and 2020, which created an infrastructure for organizing against the prime minister and even contributed to his defeat in the 2021 elections. By then, Israeli politics had been thoroughly polarized around Netanyahu and the threat he posed to democracy. But anti-Netanyahu sentiment wasn't strong enough to block him from returning to power in 2022, when he put together a coalition so far to the right that Israelis on the center and left went from very concerned to outright panicked.

So when the government unveiled its sweeping plan to overhaul the judiciary in January 2023, it led to an immediate and extraordinary public uprising. Tens of thousands of Israelis flooded the streets of Tel Aviv to demonstrate against the proposal, with protests rapidly growing and spreading across the country. In late January, more than 130 Israeli high-tech firms permitted their employees to walk out for an hour in a coordinated strike to protest the overhaul. An informal leadership committee called the Struggle HQ popped up to coordinate direct action nationwide. It organized "days of disruption" to supplement the weekly protests, during which Israelis engaged in acts of civil disobedience like shutting down highways.

When Netanyahu overreached yet again, firing Defense Minister Yoav Gallant in late March for calling on the judicial overhaul to be shelved, the protests escalated. Hundreds of thousands of Israelis marched against what they saw as yet another slide away from democracy. Trade unions staged a general strike, shutting down airport departures, coffee shops, online retail, and even Israeli embassies abroad. Netanyahu was forced to back down: he reinstated Gallant and temporarily dropped the overhaul.

The uprising led to authoritarian adaptation. Netanyahu gambled that breaking the overhaul bill into component parts would allow him to eventually get much of it through. This so-called salami-slicing approach, a favorite of Orbán's, is based on the premise that it's easier to mask the ultimate effects of a series of smaller changes than it is the effects of one big bill. The Israeli public weren't fooled—protests continued, and even intensified—but Netanyahu did manage to pass the first component of the bill, the ban on the courts' use of reasonableness, over his country's vociferous objections (polling showed that the vast majority of Israelis opposed the overhaul).

Yet the prime minister's gamble ultimately didn't pay off. Salami slicing takes time; you have to do everything in bits rather than rapidly all at once. But it was time Netanyahu didn't have. Hamas's horrific attack on October 7 erased any chance of more overhaul provisions passing in the foreseeable future—something the prime minister admitted in a late-October press conference. Then in January, Israel's Supreme Court dealt the overhaul what looked like a death blow by overturning the reasonableness ban. By initially blocking the overhaul, and then slowing down its full passage until events intervened, the protesters ended up stopping the vast bulk of the original proposal from becoming law—and buying the court time to defend itself against what was left.

This was an unusually effective example of prodemocratic organizing. It worked in part because of the immediacy of the threat. Netanyahu had overreached so brazenly that it was comparatively easy to get ordinary Israelis to feel a sense of urgency. It worked in part because the protests tapped into the core of Israel's overlapping consensus, a sense among many Israelis that the state's democratic identity is a vital part of its national character. And it worked in part because the country's overlapping consensus on democracy allowed for political diversity. The antioccupation left had its own small zone in the main Tel Aviv protest, but many centrists with more hawkish views on the Palestinian conflict marched next to them. Military reservists who vowed not to serve if the bill was passed played a crucial role in raising the alarm in the influential military establishment. While there were limits to the movement—most notably, it failed to pick up much traction among Palestinian citizens of Israel—it on the whole stands out as a striking example of a democratic civil society standing up to the reactionary spirit.

The Israeli movement, along with others like it elsewhere, contains several important lessons for prodemocracy organizing—lessons that philanthropists, activists, and even ordinary citizens can act on today. They fall into four broad buckets: building activist capacities as democracy insurance; strengthening institutions like trade unions to build democracy's grassroots; scaling up academic ideas for prodemocracy work as a kind of evidence-based democracy; and supporting innovative long-range experiments in democracy. The rest of this chapter examines each of these in turn.

Democracy Insurance

Nonviolent resistance to authoritarianism is not simply a matter of putting people on the streets. The greatest historical practitioners of nonviolence, Mahatma Gandhi and Martin Luther King Jr., emphasized that nonviolent actions need to be purposeful. They need to use tactics matched to the specific ends activists want to achieve. Nonviolent struggle is often reduced to mass protest and the changing of minds through moral example, but it also involves coercing bad actors (like Netanyahu) into conceding by inflicting costs on them. The specific tactics activists should use—including consumer boycotts, labor strikes, shutdowns of public roads, and noncooperation with government agencies—will vary from case to case.

Designing nonviolent prodemocracy campaigns is not easy. The Israeli protesters had some major advantages, including both an existing infrastructure for organizing protests and a huge and highly motivated bloc of supporters willing to go to extremes to try to stop the overhaul. Not every country will be that lucky; Israel itself acted only after Netanyahu had spent years eroding the country's democratic institutions through quieter means. People tend to be supermotivated to defend democracy only when the hour is getting late—and sometimes they oversleep their alarm.

To prevent this from happening, democracy's advocates need to institutionalize civil resistance. They must build a set of institutions that train ordinary citizens in when and how to use nonviolent action in democracy's defense, even providing opportunity for citizens to pursue prodemocracy organizing as a full-time career. This institutionalization serves two functions. First, it creates a group of people who are actively watching for incremental signs of democratic backsliding, constantly working to prevent things like salami-slicing tactics from escaping public attention. Second, it creates a cadre of experienced leaders who can organize the masses in crisis situations like what happened in Israel in 2023.

Hardy Merriman, president of the International Center on Nonviolent Conflict, described this broad concept to me as "democracy insurance." Hopefully, he said, you don't need to call on these activists much. But they are indispensable when disaster strikes.

Philanthropists can help purchase such insurance for a society by donating in ways designed with long-term institutionalization in mind. They could, for example, create a kind of "activist academy" that trains ordinary citizens in the use of nonviolent tactics to defend democracy. They could also fund fellowships or even entire organizations designed to make prodemocracy activism a more realistic career path for a greater number of people.

Democracy's Grassroots

It's important to take an expansive view of what "prodemocracy" organizing means. Many organizations that are not explicitly dedicated to defending democracy can nonetheless play an important role in supporting prodemocracy struggles. Sometimes they're even capable of addressing the deep social divisions that fuel the rise of the reactionary spirit in the first place.

The most obvious examples are organizations that directly challenge social hierarchy: movements against oppression on the basis of race, religion, ethnicity, gender, caste, and/or sexual orientation. Such organizations can of course spur a surge in the reactionary spirit; their challenges to hierarchy generally prompt resistance. But they are also an indispensable part of any long-run effort to tame the reactionary spirit's power.

Organizations that aim to improve trust between citizens also have an important role. They can build connections that make citizens less likely to view people with different political views as Schmittian enemies. Such groups include nonreactionary religious organizations, social clubs, and amateur sports leagues—the sorts of places where people can come together across social lines. Political scientists, most notably Robert Putnam, have extensively demonstrated the importance of these groups in maintaining a healthy democratic society.

Labor unions are a particularly important example. Socialists often describe unions as an example of "economic democracy": a way for workers to push back against the authoritarianism of bosses, one of the most pervasive forms of tyranny in advanced capitalist economies. Perhaps because of this impulse, unions often play an important role in building

230 | THE REACTIONARY SPIRIT

and supporting an overlapping consensus—entering into it for the benefit of the working class they represent.

The Polish trade union Solidarity famously (and ironically) had a central role in weakening and ultimately dethroning Poland's communist regime in the 1980s. In existing democratic states or competitive authoritarian ones, unions can play an important part in helping organize collective struggle against democratic erosion. We saw this clearly in the Israeli example, but also in Hungary. In 2018 and 2019, labor unions organized the largest round of antigovernment protests since Orbán's takeover. The demonstrations were kicked off by the so-called slave law, which functionally forced workers to engage in 150 additional hours of overtime per year while permitting employers to delay compensation for up to three years.

There's even evidence that unions can undermine the very foundations of reactionary politics. Research on unions in the United States by political scientists Paul Frymer and Jake Grumbach found that "white union members have lower racial resentment and greater support for policies that benefit African Americans." This doesn't appear to be incidental, the product of white people in unions being more racially progressive than average when they join. By studying the attitudes of white workers before and after they joined a union, Frymer and Grumbach demonstrated what looked a lot like a causal effect of union membership: being part of a union actually made people more racially progressive. This study suggests that something about being in a labor union—perhaps having regular contact with people of different backgrounds in a mutually supportive environment, or the general experience of engaging in class-based solidarity—actually works to weaken the reactionary spirit's power at an elemental psychological level.

This is not to say that unions are a social cure-all. Some unions can themselves become authoritarian institutions, either through a rigid hierarchical organizational structure or by corruptly aligning with a repressive regime. Some evidence shows that they can slow economic growth. Public sector shops can occasionally make government services worse or even (in the case of American police unions) enable outright oppression.

But these are surmountable problems. The evidence suggests that unions have an essential, perhaps even irreplaceable, role in democratic civil society by creating a foundation for prodemocracy activism and even by attacking the root cause of reactionary surges. Yet labor unions are in long-term decline, at least in advanced democracies: the percentage of unionized workers in countries that are part of the Organization for Economic Cooperation and Development fell from an average of 33.6 percent in 1960 to 16 percent in 2019. Working to reverse this decline—by encouraging unionization or even joining a union yourself—is an immediate and feasible step for someone interested in rebuilding a democracy's foundations.

Evidence-Based Democracy

Another important step is to strengthen a society's resources for what I call evidence-based democracy: determining which tactics for prodemocracy activism are best supported by social scientific research and then funding organizations that can implement them at scale. Today, some of the best examples of evidence-based democracy are happening in the United States.

In 2023, a group of five researchers published an important study on attitudes toward democracy among partisan Republicans and Democrats. Their findings suggest that it's possible to make even some hard-core partisans change their minds on the topic—and the researchers tested a strategy for doing so. In their first survey, they asked study participants to say how likely they were to support their party engaging in antidemocratic behavior (e.g., changing election rules to hurt the other party). They also asked participants to assess how likely they thought people on the other side would be to support such behavior. What they found was striking: both Democrats and Republicans significantly overestimated the other side's willingness to endorse antidemocratic actions. The higher their overestimations, the more likely they were to support their own party engaging in those same behaviors.

The researchers also tested whether the misperceptions could be corrected, specifically by showing participants evidence that they were overestimating just how much people on the other side were willing to break the rules. This data was persuasive for both Republicans and Democrats: after being shown that the other side was less antidemocratic than they thought, participants became less likely to support their own side breaching democratic norms. The effect was very large: in a separate "megastudy" involving thirty thousand people, the researchers found that their method "ranked first in lowering antidemocratic attitudes and first in lowering an overall composite index of all eight outcomes in the megastudy, including partisan animosity and support for partisan violence." Many Republicans, they concluded, "want to protect democracy and . . . much more so than many Democrats assume"— meaning that despite the GOP base's reactionary tilt, many Republicans remain inside America's overlapping consensus.

For this reason, the researchers recommended that Democratic leaders "focus on convincing everyday Republicans of Democrats' unwavering commitment to democracy [through] a concerted messaging campaign and credible demonstrations of this commitment." This conclusion matches what successful Democrats who were competing against election deniers did in the 2022 elections. Jocelyn Benson, the current secretary of state in Michigan, heavily focused her campaign message that year on democracy as a nonpartisan issue, not only attacking her opponent's antidemocratic credentials but positioning herself as standing for the notion that everyone deserves a right to vote regardless of who they end up voting for.

This insight applies beyond campaigns. Research on political behavior and attitudes finds that it's easiest to persuade someone when you know them personally. People generally trust people they know more than random strangers, and thus they care more about their opinions. It follows that you, reader, have the power to bolster democracy in your everyday life simply by talking to people that you know who disagree with you politically. Instead of trying to tell them that they're wrong about, let's say, abortion or affirmative action, you can simply reiterate your own commitment to democracy and democratic values. If you can persuade them that folks on your side of the aisle care about respecting their side's right to compete fairly, evidence suggests that they'll become less likely to endorse a destructive authoritarian like Trump.

Political scientists have also found more effective ways to address the foundations of reactionary politics: the deep-seated attachment to social hierarchy and prejudices about out-groups that powers the reactionary spirit around the world. In 2008, an LGBT activist in Los Angeles named Dave Fleischer began studying why a majority of Californians had just voted to criminalize same-sex marriage in a state-wide ballot referendum. He found that the best strategy for changing their minds was to listen to their concerns, take them seriously, and then share his personal experiences as a gay man in an attempt to demonstrate his own humanity. This attempt to connect with his political opponents through empathy proved remarkably effective—far more so than engaging in heated abstract arguments about human rights or religion.

Fleischer named the approach "deep canvassing," and his organization, Leadership Lab, began implementing it on a larger scale. In the years since, political scientists have rigorously studied deep canvassing as a persuasion technique; after some missteps, most notably an infamous paper with extensively faked data, the results have been quite positive. Deep canvassing has been shown to reduce targets' levels of hostility toward both transgender Americans and undocumented immigrants at levels few other interventions can match. Some organizations, like the Deep Canvass Institute, are attempting to build on the Leadership Lab's model and implement deep-canvassing campaigns at scale.

The process is both time consuming and expensive, as deep canvassers need training to properly conduct an empathetic conversation. This is where philanthropists can help. Devoting more funding toward efforts to scale up deep canvassing could play a significant role in reducing the negative social attitudes on which the reactionary spirit feeds, thereby making the kind of proactive, positive change that's necessary to actually strengthen democracy's foundations.

Experiments in Democracy

As much as we know about techniques for prodemocracy action, there's a lot more that we don't know. The study of democratic backsliding is still in its infancy, especially when it comes to understanding backsliding in long-standing and wealthy democracies. So it's essential for people to try new tactics to see what might work—including undertaking really ambitious proposals that might not pay off.

An organization called Keseb is supporting democratic experimentation at a global scale. In 2023, Keseb released a report on how to make multiracial democracy work, based on interviews with over seventy-five activists in the United States, Brazil, South Africa, and India. One of the group's core conclusions from the interviews was that activists feel isolated. Whereas reactionary authoritarians often study and learn from each other, democracy activists have few formal opportunities to learn from people working on similar issues in other countries. To that end, Keseb has created a fellowship program designed to bring prodemocracy activists from around the world together and provide them funding to expand their work back home.

The results of these various grants may not be visible for some time. Some of them may have little impact; some may have immeasurable impact. Keseb's CEO, Yordanos Eyoel, told me that thinking about impact on democracy as something you can immediately quantify is a mistake. "It is important for us to shift from 'Is this an efficient way to convert voters on specific things' to 'How are we changing the culture of democracy?'"

To this end, Eyoel argued, the "most important thing we need to do [is] define what an inspiring democracy looks like in the twenty-first century." This isn't a question of message-testing political slogans, at least not at this stage. It's about connecting with citizens in democratic societies at a deep level to understand what they feel is lacking in their societies and what kind of substantive vision for the future would motivate them to get involved in prodemocratic political work.

This kind of talk may sound handwavy or utopian. Many people have proposed new visions for democracy, none of which seem to have provided a way out of our current reactionary crisis. It may even seem a little self-justifying, an excuse for organizations like Keseb to keep going when their work yields little in the way of obvious practical results. But we are in the middle of dealing with a threat that is both old (the reactionary spirit) and relatively new (a global antidemocratic movement that claims to be acting in democracy's defense). There has never been a challenge exactly like this before. It follows that some of the responses we need will be completely new too. Developing a novel vision for twenty-first-century democracy is *hard*. It makes sense to try a number of different tacks and see which ones yield results over the course of years.

In the meantime, the fight will take place in the trenches. Reactionaries will attempt to advance their agendas without triggering a backlash while democracy's supporters will work to expose them and attack the foundations of their political support in public. The struggle won't be easy, and there is no guarantee of victory.

Still, over the past century, democracy's champions have racked up a pretty good track record. We ought to take heart—and some lessons—from their example.

CONCLUSION

Carl Schmitt was not the only German thinker whose work captured an enduring aspect of the reactionary spirit. In the late nineteenth century, around the time that Schmitt was born, Friedrich Nietzsche developed a critique of democracy that tells us something essential about what makes reactionary politics tick today.

Nietzsche was both a brilliant and a deeply strange philosopher, his oft-cryptic writing admitting of many radically different interpretations. He is perhaps best known for his extreme attack on the Christian ethical tradition, which he blamed for replacing the celebration of individual achievement and greatness with a "slave morality" that valorized weakness and timidity. This is not the kind of rhetoric you hear from Western reactionary leaders today, who often count conservative church leaders as some of their key supporters.

Yet Nietzsche's related attack on democracy—that as "the inheritance of the Christian movement," it was a political system that debased what is great and beautiful in the human spirit—speaks to something that runs through the bloodstream of the contemporary reactionary right. Nietzsche's disdain for the incremental and compromising nature of democratic politics—he decried its "restlessness, emptiness, and noisy wranglings"—captures an important *psychological* element of how the reactionary spirit expresses itself today.

Liberal democracy, Nietzsche wrote in *Twilight of the Idols* (1889), makes "people small, cowardly, and pleasure-loving—with liberal institutions, the herd animal is victorious every time." He believed that there was "no more poisonous poison" than "the doctrine of equality," that "wrong never lies in unequal rights" but rather "lies in the assertion of 'equal' rights." Political institutions cannot be sustained by consent of the governed but rather through "a kind of will [that is] anti-liberal to the point of malice." It was in figures like Napoleon, "the heir of a stronger, longer, older civilization," that Nietzsche saw glimpses of what politics should truly be.

Modern reactionaries have tapped into this Nietzschean well. For a certain segment of their supporters, figures like Trump and Modi are not just political leaders but national saviors with almost superhuman qualities. While it's not unheard of for democratic politicians to develop devout personal fandoms, there's a different emotional core to it in reactionary politics: one premised on an almost spiritual sense that the great leader can, through sheer personal strength, smash the boundaries of ordinary politics. Here is a man—this is all bound up with gender—who has come to lead *us* in a triumphant march against *them*. After Modi ordered airstrikes on alleged terrorist bases in Pakistan in 2019, his chief deputy, Amit Shah, bragged that only "a man with a 56-inch chest" could take such aggressive action to protect India's security—a commonly repeated boast, in BJP circles, about the prime minister's virility.

"The leader's displays of machismo [project] the idea that he is above laws that others must follow," the historian

Ruth Ben-Ghiat wrote in her book *Strongmen*. "Picking up on powerful resentments, hopes, and fears, they present themselves as the vehicle for obtaining what is most wanted, whether it is territory, safety from racial others, securing male authority, or payback for exploitation by internal or external enemies."

This is a politics of emotional gratification that exploits an unsatisfying truth about democracy. In democratic politics, you typically compromise with your enemy rather than vanquish them. Victories are generally partial and incremental rather than sweeping and total; relinquishing power is an inevitability. In reactionary politics, the grubbiness of democratic life is washed away by the glorious huzzahs of the group, with the manly leader as its focus. Politics is not merely a way to manage collective problems, but a form of existential struggle that gives members of the friend group a sense of purpose and meaning.

Nietzsche challenges us to consider whether life in a stable democracy is simply too *boring* to last. Does democracy sap politics of the vigor, the conflict, the heroism that make it vital? The answer to this question, I think, is a resounding no. And the reasons why should give us some much-needed hope about democracy's future.

THE QUIET SOURCE OF DEMOCRATIC STRENGTH

Nietzsche did not believe that societies should be judged by how well they provide for the needs and well-being of their citizens. This is liberal-democratic pablum. Instead, he believed, politics is about the ennobling of citizens—specifically, those elect citizens whose extraordinary character allows them to be ennobled in the first place. Superior people and nations are forged through the crucible of violent, existential struggle, a kind of conflict alien to democratic life.

"The peoples who were worth something, who became worthy, never became worthy under liberal institutions," he wrote in *Twilight of the Idols*. "*Great danger* made them into something that deserves respect, danger, which first teaches us to get to know the means at our disposal, our virtues, our defense and weapons, our own spirit—danger, which forces us to be strong." Nietzsche here is positioning political conflict as valuable in itself. The act of fighting and winning, of asserting your will on your supine enemies, helps individuals not only become stronger but be the very best version of themselves. "One has relinquished great life when one relinquishes war," he wrote.

Many modern reactionaries share this vision, albeit in more group-oriented form. The purpose of political struggle is not for individuals to find their personal greatness, but to find meaning through belonging to a collective—and helping it triumph in its struggle against its enemies. This is an important, and not widely understood, element of the Trump phenomenon.

It is often noted that Trump seems to have few, if any, concrete policy positions or ideological principles, and that his followers will generally go along with whatever he decides he stands for in the moment. There are many reasons why he gets away with this shiftiness, but a big one is that Trump's hard-core base sees the MAGA movement itself as more important than the actual wielding of power.

I didn't fully grasp this point until I read a column in the *New York Times* by David French, a Never-Trump conservative who lives in a midsize town in Tennessee, about what he termed the "joy" of the MAGA movement. Describing scenes of camaraderie and laughter at Trump rallies and boat parades, he pointed out that Democrats who see Trumpism as a purely rage-driven phenomenon miss the kindness with which the Trump people treat each other. We focus on the antagonism between friend and enemy in Schmittian politics, but we don't think nearly as much about relations *between* friends—and how much it matters for people to identify who their friends truly are.

Trump events "give MAGA devotees a sense of *belonging*," French wrote. "They see a country that's changing around them and they are uncertain about their place in it. But they *know* they have a place at a Trump rally, surrounded by others—overwhelmingly white, many evangelical—who feel the same way they do."

To build a politics of reactionary vitality, you need this level of energy—or something like it. But although some people are looking for meaning in politics in this way, they're almost certainly a small minority. Only 37 percent of Americans voted in all three of the last general elections (2018, 2020, and 2022). In 2016, the last year both major parties had competitive presidential primaries, only 28.5 percent of eligible voters bothered to vote in one. It is safe to say that the percentage of Americans who are deeply involved in politics on a day-to-day basis, seeing participation in political life as a major source of meaning for themselves personally, is considerably lower than either of those figures.

The hard-core Trumpists French described are unusual in that way. Other Americans' alienation from their brand of enthusiastic extremism—that is, their perception that Trump and his followers threatened American normalcy and stability—is part of why Joe Biden managed to beat Trump in 2020.

The MAGA movement's isolation speaks to a larger truth. For most people, politics isn't about the joy of struggle or the vitality of conquest; it's about making sure they're able to live the kind of life they really want. They care first and foremost about their families, their careers, their hobbies—things that are, by and large, only indirectly related to the struggle for political power. Most people don't live for politics; they engage in politics to live.

This is partly why democracy (and liberalism) works so well. Democracy doesn't demand that people make politics the centerpiece of their life; it asks only that they make themselves heard if and when doing so matters to them. True meaning is found elsewhere, with democracy as an enabler—a guarantee that people will be respected, protected from being crushed, and given an equal chance to advocate for their interests. What people really want is private freedom and public voice. Liberal democracy provides both.

Nietzsche scorned "the contemptible sort of wellbeing dreamt of by grocers, Christians, cows, women, Englishmen, and other democrats." In doing so, he missed something that reactionary authoritarians characteristically miss: democracy's protection of "contemptible" comfort breeds social strength. A brand of reactionary politics built on passion guarantees instability. In seeking out monsters to destroy and witches to burn, it bucks against the institutions of everyday life that most people value. They resent when political developments threaten their "contemptible sort of wellbeing," and they're willing to fight for it.

There is a reason that the most successful modern reactionary, Viktor Orbán, never really depended on passion or perceptions of manly vitality for political success. Orbán knew that trying to politicize life *too much* would lead people to resent him, inviting a backlash from those who would (for the most part) rather not think about politics at all. So he built his competitive authoritarian state as quietly as he could, and he tried to make its repressive operation as invisible and unobtrusive as possible. By institutionalizing his politics, taking it out of the realm of passion and into the cold kingdom of bureaucracy, Orbán created an authoritarian system that could conceivably last for years.

The politics of passion, by contrast, is often fleeting. So obsessed with image and energy, its proponents overestimate how well the energies they've harnessed can be sustained—and how widely they're shared.

Nietzsche saw but one country on the European continent worthy of his admiration: czarist Russia, which he described as "the only power that has physical endurance today, that can wait, that can still promise something." The czars' stubborn holdout against the democratizing tide sweeping the West was, in his mind, a sign of a great Russian future.

Had Nietzsche lived past 1900, he would have been disappointed. The czarist regime forever lagged behind western Europe in military clout, economic development, and scientific innovation. Its final years in power were defined by humiliating military failures in the Russo-Japanese War and then in World War I, the latter of which led directly to its toppling in the Russian Revolution. It seemed that Nietzsche's enthusiasm for the czars was not representative of how most Russians experienced life under them.

If a thinker as luminous as Nietzsche could make such an embarrassing misjudgment, then surely others could fall into the same trap. And indeed they did. In case after case throughout modern history, observers would predict that the strength and masculine energy of authoritarian politics would allow it

244 I THE REACTIONARY SPIRIT

to outmuscle and outcompete democracies—in war, politics, and commerce. Again and again, these predictions would be embarrassed by events.

In her book *The Machine Has a Soul*, historian Katy Hull examined some especially striking examples: four prominent interwar Americans who became infatuated with Italian fascism in the 1920s. A common theme in these fascist sympathizers' writing was that the United States had fallen prey to a social crisis—both a deep disillusionment with the messy interest-group politics of twentieth-century democracy, and a spiritual emptiness that hollowed out the souls of Americans in the materialistic Roaring Twenties. "We have invented and found nearly everything; about the only thing we have not found is ourselves," lamented Richard Washburn Child, the US ambassador to Italy during Mussolini's rise to power.

Child and his comrades came to view American democracy as a "broken-down machine that could not be fixed," in Hull's summary. They looked to Italy as a source of renewal, seeing fascism not only as a more efficient political model but as one that could address the yawning chasm at the center of the American heart. Child praised the "lyric and epic quality" of fascist politics, crediting the ideology with making "an extraordinary contribution to the whole world by raising ideals of human courage, discipline, and responsibility." He was also personally infatuated with Mussolini, going so far as to edit the dictator's English-language autobiography (titled *My Autobiography*). In the foreword, Child described Il Duce as a man who "gives the impression of an energy which cannot be bottled, which bubbles up and over like an eternally effervescent, irrepressible fluid."

Child's paeans to fascism were wild exaggerations even based on what people knew at the time. They look far worse now, when Mussolini is remembered less as a font of energy than as Hitler's incompetent sidekick. From the contemporary vantage point, the notion that anyone would see Italian fascism as the exemplar of a spiritually healthy society is absurd—let alone when compared with American democracy, which produced a nation that would dominate the latter half of the twentieth century.

Though Child came not even close to Nietzsche's intellectual level, the two men fell into remarkably similar errors: overestimating both the degree to which democracy bred weakness and the degree to which authoritarian alternatives were sources of strength. Their obsession with the seeming emptiness of democracy, and the majestic power of its authoritarian rivals, gets the source of political durability exactly backward. It is democracy, in all its grubbiness, that best meets people where they are—and thus best gives them what they want.

This is why, despite all the evidence of the reactionary spirit's resurgence, I'm still guardedly optimistic about democracy's future.

Predictions of its imminent doom, of its obsolescence in the face of authoritarian challenge, have repeatedly proven wrong for the last two hundred years. Offering such predictions today risks confusing what *is* happening with what *will* happen. The passionate fires of reaction could, and quite possibly will, dwindle to embers. Democracy taps into something more permanent, more essential even than the distinction between friend and enemy: each person's desire to have a good life. Democracy's supporters are legion; if they wake up to the reactionary threat in sufficient numbers, they will be unstoppable.

But this awakening is by no means inevitable. Democracy as we understand it, founded on the idea of essential human equality, has existed for but a blink of the eye in historical terms. Past reactionaries have failed to overthrow it not due to some iron law of history, but because they faced determined opposition from democracy's champions. Today's reactionaries, by presenting themselves as democrats, are doing their best to avoid inciting a similar level of resistance.

The contest for democracy's future is thus different in some respects from the one previous generations faced, but at its heart the struggle is the same. It is a conflict over whether democracy's champions are as committed to equality as its rivals are to hierarchy. Previous generations of democrats showed that they were up to the challenge. The great question facing all of us today is whether we are.

ACKNOWLEDGMENTS

It takes a lot of work to make a book into a real thing—more than I thought when I started writing this one. But I was lucky to have an exceptional team helping me through the process of becoming a first-time author.

Things really started when Greg Shaw connected me with my agent, Jim Levine. Attending a wedding with Greg, I showed him one of the earliest outlines of what would become *The Reactionary Spirit*. Greg set up a call to discuss it with Jim, who had already talked over some worse ideas I had for books—and Jim was gracious enough to listen.

Jim then set up a meeting with Clive Priddle, the publisher at PublicAffairs, helping me to sell him on the book. Clive and his team have been excellent throughout, providing top-notch editing and hand-holding through the process of turning a manuscript into a book. In addition to superb lead editor Clive, I want to thank Jaime Leifer, Kiyo Sasso, Johanna Dickson, Pete Garceau, Kelley Blewster, and Shena Redmond—all of whom played important roles in bringing this book to life and getting it out into the world.

He's not at PublicAffairs, but I also want to single out my fact-checker (and former *Vox* colleague) Cameron Peters for doing an exceptional job being my safety net. Any factual errors that remain are mine and not his.

One of the great pleasures of being a journalist is that you don't just have to rely on yourself. You send an email or pick up a phone, and some of the very brightest people in the world will share their insights with you for free. Conversations with many, many such people have informed this book's argument—but a handful went above and beyond.

Steven Levitsky, Jake Grumbach, Cas Mudde, Corey Robin, Dahlia Scheindlin, and Kim Lane Scheppele all read early drafts and provided invaluable feedback in their respective areas of expertise. Joshua Cohen, Jan-Werner Müller, and Seva Gunitsky gracefully talked about some core ideas with me. My obvious intellectual debt to John Rawls is also owed to David Estlund, John Tomasi, Sharon Krause, and Charles Larmore—my college professors who left me with a conviction that Rawls got something big right. The overall argument is stronger for their influence.

Many people at *Vox* deserve a mention here. My editors Elbert Ventura and Patrick Reis were exceptionally patient, even affirmatively helpful, in assisting me in balancing my daytime responsibilities with the need to write a book. My colleague and (more importantly) friend Libby Nelson spent her free time reading the book and providing suggestions. Libby, my dear friend Dylan Matthews, and the others in our original *Vox* family—Andrew Prokop, German Lopez, and Dara Lind—are the best colleagues and friends I could have asked for. I also owe a lot to *Vox*'s editors-in-chief, past and present: Ezra Klein, Lauren Williams, and Swati Sharma. They encouraged me to swing for the fences and become the kind of journalist who could write a book like this.

The Pulitzer Center on Crisis Reporting and Shalom Hartman Institute both supported my field reporting abroad. Some of the book's core arguments were debuted at presentations to the Patriots and Pragmatists group and the University of

Nebraska's Sommerhauser Symposium on Holocaust Education, and subsequently refined.

My friends James Brockway and Paul Rogerson both provided helpful feedback at various stages of the process. When I was describing the book's argument to Paul one night, he told me that the concept of "the reactionary spirit" would make for a good title. He was right.

My parents, Tom Beauchamp and Ruth Faden, are not just subjects in the book: they are intellectual titans in their own right. Their feedback on the manuscript was helpful, as was their help with childcare during the drafting process. But their real influence came in a lifetime of moral and intellectual education. I am who I am because of you two; I hope you're proud.

Thank you to my sister Karine Fiore, her husband, Rich, and their children Samuel, Mateo, Alex, and Anna. My life is better for all of you being in it.

Finally, Katelyn Esmonde—a brilliant scholar and extraordinary wife. Her feedback on the manuscript, while valuable, was the least of her contributions.

Katie not only talked over my thoughts on the book over the course of years, but helped me through periods of angst when I thought I would never get this done. When I was feeling down, she understood what I needed to cheer me up (noodles and beer, for the most part). When I needed to write on nights and weekends, she by necessity picked up the slack when it came to childcare and household labor. As someone who has spent the last two-hundred-odd pages preaching the virtues of equality, I've put quite a lot of red on my marital ledger. I hope to pay out to Katie over a lifetime together with our children, Ellie and Daveed Esmonde-Beauchamp. They didn't contribute to the book even a little bit, but they have contributed everything to our lives simply by existing.

SELECTED
BIBLIOGRAPHY

Acharya, Avidit, Matthew Blackwell, and Maya Sen. *Deep Roots: How Slavery Still Shapes Southern Politics*. Princeton, NJ: Princeton University Press, 2018.

Anderson, Carol. *White Rage: The Unspoken Truth of Our Racial Divide*. New York: Bloomsbury USA, 2016.

Ben-Ghiat, Ruth. *Strongmen: Mussolini to the Present*. New York: W. W. Norton, 2021.

Cowie, Jefferson. *Freedom's Dominion: A Saga of White Resistance to Federal Power*. New York: Basic Books, 2022.

Fukuyama, Francis. *The End of History and the Last Man*. New York: Free Press, 2006.

Golwalkar, M. S. *We, or Our Nationhood Defined*. Nagpur: Bharat Publishing, 1939.

Grumbach, Jake. *Laboratories Against Democracy: How National Parties Transformed State Politics*. Princeton, NJ: Princeton University Press, 2022.

Guha, Ramachandra. *India After Gandhi: The History of the World's Largest Democracy*. London: Pan MacMillan, 2017.

Gunitsky, Seva. *Aftershocks: Great Powers and Domestic Reforms in the Twentieth Century*. Princeton, NJ: Princeton University Press, 2017.

Guriev, Sergei, and Daniel Treisman. *Spin Dictators: The Changing Face of Tyranny in the 21st Century*. Princeton, NJ: Princeton University Press, 2022.

Hacker, Jacob, and Paul Pierson. *Let Them Eat Tweets: How the Right Rules in an Age of Extreme Inequality*. New York: Liveright, 2020.

Hull, Katy. *The Machine Has a Soul: American Sympathy with Italian Fascism*. Princeton, NJ: Princeton University Press, 2021.

Jaffrelot, Christophe. *Modi's India: Hindu Nationalism and the Rise of Ethnic Democracy*. Translated by Cynthia Schoch. Princeton, NJ: Princeton University Press, 2021.

Kahane, Meir. *They Must Go*. New York: Beta Nu, 2019.

Khilnani, Sunil. *The Idea of India*. New York: Farrar, Straus, and Giroux, 2017.

Lindsay, J. H., ed. *Report of the Proceedings and Debates of the Constitutional Convention of the State of Virginia*. Richmond: Hermitage Press, 1906.

Mehta, Pratap Bhanu. *The Burden of Democracy*. New York: Penguin, 2017.

Mickey, Robert. *Paths out of Dixie: The Democratization of Authoritarian Enclaves in America's Deep South 1944–1972*. Princeton, NJ: Princeton University Press, 2015.

Neiman, Susan. *Learning from the Germans: Race and the Memory of Evil*. New York: Farrar, Straus, and Giroux, 2019.

Nietzsche, Friedrich. *Beyond Good and Evil*. Translated by R. J. Hollingdale. New York: Penguin Classics, 2003.

Nietzsche, Friedrich. *Twilight of the Idols: Or, How to Philosophize with the Hammer*. Translated by Richard Polt. Indianapolis: Hackett, 1997.

Norris, Pippa, and Ronald Inglehart. *Cultural Backlash: Trump, Brexit, and Authoritarian Populism*. Cambridge, UK: Cambridge University Press, 2019.

Rawls, John. *Political Liberalism*. New York: Columbia University Press, 2005.

Rawls, John. *A Theory of Justice*. Cambridge, MA: Harvard University Press, 1971.

Robin, Corey. *The Reactionary Mind*. Oxford, UK: Oxford University Press, 2017.

Scheindlin, Dahlia. *The Crooked Timber of Democracy in Israel*. London: De Gruyter, 2023.

Schmitt, Carl. *The Concept of the Political*. Translated by George Schwab. Chicago: University of Chicago Press, 2008.

Schmitt, Carl. *The Crisis of Parliamentary Democracy*. Translated by Ellen Kennedy. Cambridge, MA: MIT Press, 1985.

Tesler, Michael. *Post-Racial or Most-Racial? Race and Politics in the Obama Era*. Chicago: University of Chicago Press, 2016.

Tocqueville, Alexis de. *Democracy in America*, vol. 1. Translated by Henry Reeve. London: Saunders and Otley, 1835.

Ziblatt, Daniel. *Conservative Parties and the Birth of Democracy*. Cambridge, UK: Cambridge University Press, 2017.

INDEX

elections *(continued)*
US, 23–24, 199, 203–205, 207,
218–222, 233, 241
voting, 18, 21, 26, 49, 50, 53, 77,
98–99, 124–125, 241
Electoral College, abolishing, 207
Eliyahu, Amihai, 160–161
El Salvador, 191–192
"end of history," 4, 90
England, 38–39, 163
Enyedi, Zsolt, 121
EPP (European People's Party), 130
equality, 172, 184. *See also* inequalities
disposable, 153, 154
dissatisfaction with, 90, 95, 173
as vaccine against reactionary spirit,
203
Erinnerungskultur ("memory culture"),
71
ethnic cleansing, of Palestinians, 146,
160
ethnic democracy, 139–145, 164
Eurobarometer survey, 121
European People's Party (EPP), 130
European Union, 23, 112–113, 119,
126, 130–131, 187–188
evidence-based democracy, 227,
231–234
exclusion, weaponizing, 207
experiments, in democracy, 227,
234–236
Eyoel, Yordanos, 235

far-right (extreme) parties, 16, 25, 74,
189–190, 202, 209. *See also specific
political parties*
fertile ground for, 91–94, 99, 101
politics and, 1, 12, 14–15, 37, 85–89,
90–92, 140, 155–157, 163, 179
fascism, 6, 74–75, 81, 85, 87, 117,
155
communism and, 24, 80, 89, 184
"Indian version of," 171
Italian, 17–18, 80, 244–245
Fernandez Ancona, Jen, 221
Fidesz party, Hungary, 104–105,
107–127, 130, 151, 223
Fields, Barbara, 40–41
Financial Times (newspaper), 189
Finchem, Mark, 203–204

Finkelstein, Arthur, 118
Fleischer, David, 233–234
FN (Front National, National Rally),
France, 85–88, 92
Fontes, Adrian, 203–205
Foreign Affairs (magazine), 164
Fox News, 106
FPÖ (Freedom Party), Austria, 87, 90
France, 13, 85–88, 92, 168
Frederick Douglass Republicans, 2
Freedom Party (FPÖ), Austria, 87, 90
free speech, 29–30, 51, 90
French, David, 240–241
French Revolution, 17, 75, 199
Front National (FN, National Rally),
France, 85–88, 92
Frymer, Paul, 230
Fugitive Slave Act, 162
Fukuyama, Francis, 90, 95
funding, 112, 181, 187
political parties, 50–51, 113, 114
prodemocracy activism, 231, 234, 235

Gallant, Yoav, 225
Gandhi, Indira, 175
Gandhi, Mahatma, 170, 172–173, 180,
227
Gandhi, Rahul, 167–168
Garrison, William Lloyd, 43
"Gays for Trump," 33, 34
Geller, Pamela, 34
gender, 60, 63, 99–100, 122
General Assembly, UN, 21
George III (King of England), 40
Germany, 17–18, 69–74, 91, 94, 119,
130, 171. *See also* Nazis
gerrymander, 6, 20, 62–63, 109–110,
114
Getmansky, Anna, 149
Gharib family, 133–134
Gibson, Edward, 51
Glass, Carter, 52–53, 66, 68
Godse, Nathuram, 172–173
Golder, Matt, 87
Goldstein, Baruch, 147, 148, 156
Golwalkar, M. S., 170–172, 174, 178
Google, 112
GOP. *See* Republican Party
grassroots, of democracy, 227, 229–231
Great Britain, 13, 83

Zack Beauchamp is a senior correspondent at *Vox*, where he covers challenges to democracy in the United States and abroad, right-wing populism, and the world of ideas. He has received funding awards from the Pulitzer Center on Crisis Reporting to report in the field on democratic decline in Israel and Hungary, and was the longtime host of *Worldly*, *Vox*'s weekly podcast on foreign policy and international affairs. He has appeared on a wide range of television and radio networks, including MSNBC, CNN, Fox News, NPR, BBC, CBC, ABC (Australia), and Al Jazeera.

Before joining *Vox*, he edited TP Ideas, a section of ThinkProgress devoted to the ideas shaping our political world. He has a master's of science from the London School of Economics in international relations and grew up in Washington, DC, where he currently lives with his wife, two children, and (rescue) dogs.

PublicAffairs is a publishing house founded in 1997. It is a tribute to the standards, values, and flair of three persons who have served as mentors to countless reporters, writers, editors, and book people of all kinds, including me.

I. F. STONE, proprietor of *I. F. Stone's Weekly*, combined a commitment to the First Amendment with entrepreneurial zeal and reporting skill and became one of the great independent journalists in American history. At the age of eighty, Izzy published *The Trial of Socrates*, which was a national bestseller. He wrote the book after he taught himself ancient Greek.

BENJAMIN C. BRADLEE was for nearly thirty years the charismatic editorial leader of *The Washington Post*. It was Ben who gave the *Post* the range and courage to pursue such historic issues as Watergate. He supported his reporters with a tenacity that made them fearless and it is no accident that so many became authors of influential, best-selling books.

ROBERT L. BERNSTEIN, the chief executive of Random House for more than a quarter century, guided one of the nation's premier publishing houses. Bob was personally responsible for many books of political dissent and argument that challenged tyranny around the globe. He is also the founder and longtime chair of Human Rights Watch, one of the most respected human rights organizations in the world.

·   ·   ·

For fifty years, the banner of Public Affairs Press was carried by its owner Morris B. Schnapper, who published Gandhi, Nasser, Toynbee, Truman, and about 1,500 other authors. In 1983, Schnapper was described by *The Washington Post* as "a redoubtable gadfly." His legacy will endure in the books to come.

Peter Osnos, *Founder*